equidistant

2018 POETRY COLLECTION

by Eric Nixon

Cover image and design by Eric Nixon.

Author photo by Kari Chapin.

ISBN-13: 978-0-9984362-3-4
BISAC: Poetry / American / General

Published by Double Yolk Press in Northampton, Massachusetts.
EricNixonAuthor@gmail.com
EricNixon.net

DEDICATION

This book is dedicated to the source of my inspiration. I don't know where it comes from, but it is always there, giving me more than I could ever use. Thank you.

AUTHOR'S FOREWARD

Another year, another collection of poetry.

Probably partially as a result of 2018 being a terrible year nationally, I focused inward and spent most of the year writing poetry (this is my third-largest collection to date), and writing my next novel, *2493: The Death Of Bryn Struse*. The novel is still being written, and knowing my glacial pace when it comes to works of fiction, it will probably be quite some time before it's actually published. That being said, I hope it happens in late 2019. My poetry collection, on the other hand, is ready; more or less on schedule.

Looking over the table of contents for this collection, you'll see a noticeable hole for the months of March and April. That lack of poetry was the result of packing, and then moving, from the uncomfortable rural Illinois town we lived in, back "home" to the joyfully relaxing Pioneer Valley of western Massachusetts. Landing back here felt like putting on your favorite comfy after-work clothes before parking it on the couch to binge-watch several seasons of your most beloved show. Every aspect of it here has re-affirmed how much we love this place.

2018 also saw me do something I've never done before: I started submitting my poetry to different journals and magazines. None were accepted, but it's something I'm going to continue with in 2019 solely because it would be nice to see my work in a magazine. That, and I'd like my huge pile of poetry (1,175 poems spread across my nine collections) to start being read by a wider audience.

This past year also saw one of my poems appear again (for the second time!) on *The Writer's Almanac*. Much like a Star Baker after a winning day of baking in the tent on *The Great British Bake Off*, I am quite chuffed to be able to listen to Garrison Keillor read my poetry.

I also joined a writing group, which has been a wonderful resource. It has given me a nice dedicated time to focus solely on writing without distractions, and the socialization aspect of it with other local writers has been great, and very informative. When I first joined and told them I wrote both poetry and science fiction novels, they asked if I wrote science fiction poetry. I incredulously responded, "Uh, *no*," like they were big ol' dummies. *But*, that got me thinking about the possibility of writing sci-fi poetry, so to challenge myself I wrote a couple ("Slicing Saturn," and "The Grounding Pull," [both found in this book under August]). I really enjoyed it and will be writing more in the future.

Oh, I almost forgot. The title of this collection is in reference to my turning 45 in 2019 and how, age-wise, I'll be at the midway point between 30 and 60. Approaching 45, and really, truly, middle aged has really given me pause because, gee whiz, I really don't feel like I'm anywhere near that old (but I guess I am). Anyway, it's had a big impact on me so now you have to read about it.

Speaking of which, it's time for me to stop writing and for you to get reading.

Please enjoy and thank you!

Eric

TABLE OF CONTENTS

The Momentum Of Existence
You Can Tell The Tourists
Meant To Be Hidden
The Wind Wasn't Refreshing
The Old American Dream
The New American Dream
Peak Summer
A Hot Dog On A Hot Day

Sunflower Tree
A Repeated Vision
My Eyes Are Rich
Everywhere And Everywhen
I Want That Knowing
So Dark So Early
Nature And Man Conspired To Censor
Poking That Bear
The Then And Gone
The Things That Mattered
Salmon To Peach
Walking On Eggshells
A New Version Is Needed

October – 10 poems
I Misread A Flyer
All It Takes Is A Month To Change Your Beliefs
Late To Its Own Funeral
AllOneWord
Trapped In A Purgatorial Place
Almost
The Noise
All The People
Backup
This Autumnal Season

November – 14 poems
Equidistant
Yesterday Flew By
Putting The Lunch Before The Holiday
The Bridge
Late At Night
Now That The Meal Is Over
Quickly Strung
Present Imbalance
Tricky Indeed
In This Particularly Odiferous Moment

In The Quiet Space
Is It About Me?
Slipping Between The Seconds
Staring Down His Driveway

December – 24 poems
Most Awards
When The Outside Better Matches The Words
Despite The Emphasis
The List Of My Superpowers
My Sink Does This Thing
A Quick Review
The Ultimate In Contrast
You Don't Yawn In Your Sleep
All Those Long-Gone Months
Protocol And Paperwork
New Traditions Through Technology
All It Takes Is An Instant
So Much Energy
Spanning The Tapering Months
We Are Hapless
It's All Planned Out
The Same Complex Coin
Speaking In Similes
The Magnetic One
Last Night
Tomorrow Will Be The Same
The Hardest Part
Stop Rowing
New Year's Eve Way Of Seeing Things

2018 total: 150

JANUARY

New Year's Day Way Of Seeing Things

We arose at 2:30 am
On New Year's Day
We left at 3:30 am
Driving east for three hours
In the dark, frigid, -14 degree night
Strangely devoid of other vehicles
As we arrived at the airport
We saw the full moon
Hanging huge and low
Perched on the horizon
Like something out of
A photography magazine
After I dropped her off
And hugged our goodbyes
I started on the three hours
Between there and home
But this time I enjoyed
The luxurious dawning light
Painting the edges of everything
In soothing, easy pastels
Giving me my very own special
New Year's Day way of seeing things
Where the road belonged to me
And with each mile, the Sun
Illuminated something new
Or tinted a building
In some fresh sparkling way
Reflecting the Golden Hour light on
Mirror-windowed office buildings
Allowing me to see the beauty
Of the first sunrise of the year
Erupting vividly behind me
Almost as if nature had agreed
With The Universe to give me
An unexpected treat
To pivot my mindset
And give me appreciation

January 1, 2018
Galena, Illinois

Midwestern Philosophy

When you start paying attention to actions
And disregard the irrelevant phrases and words
A consistent pattern begins to develop
On the behavioral patterns for this region
A Midwestern Philosophy translated
Into a simply concise phrase: "Go around me."
A belief that seems to be stronger and deeper
Than faith professed through Facebook repostings
Which is easily observed several times a minute
In any parking lot, supermarket, or big box store
Where the person in question, gets in the way,
And without looking, stops fully and completely,
Blocking your path, and if they happen to notice,
They'll shrug and give you a lazily enacted motion,
Waiving you to go around them,
As if you're the problem
And that's the problem
Again and again, over and over,
Every minute of every time I venture out in public

January 3, 2018
Galena, Illinois

Maybe this is more of a national problem of people being
completely oblivious of people around them and not giving a shit
how their actions impact others, but I have only noticed it being a
very consistent issue here in the Midwest. It's utterly maddening.

A Simple Thought, An Immediate Answer

A simple thought:
If we had won the jackpot
Of either multi-state lotteries
Where in the entire country
Would we want to own a house?

I asked both myself and my wife
This question, which brought about
An immediate answer,
In unison, of a city
Back in Massachusetts
Where we'd already lived
For several years
And was the clear favorite
Of any place we've been

That answer then caused us
Some deeper soul-searching
And an instinctively led us
To consider this question:
Why are we still living here?

> January 4, 2018
> Galena, Illinois

HA! I wrote 2018 without even thinking about it.

Also, we're going to be moving away from here in the spring. It's a fine town; very pretty and nice, but that niceness is merely window dressing and has no depth. That, and this area lacks many of the conveniences we require (dependable Internet, good supermarkets, a community of like-minded people, etc).

The War On Christmas

The war on Christmas
Is successfully waged
So completely
And successfully
This time of the year
As the remnants
Of the holiday
Don't stand a chance
Against the calendar
And the distance
From the day

January 9, 2018
Galena, Illinois

I took down my outdoor Christmas lights today, which got me thinking that no matter how much people love the holiday/the season/Jesus/pretty lights/etc. they always take down the decorations within a week or so of the new year.

The Perspective Of Distance

When something happens
Often you are much too close
Or still in the midst
Of the life changing event
To be able to do anything
Properly about it
Either way
Emotions tend to wield
Full power over you
And the voice of reason
Is unable to interrupt
Is unable to compete
Because the crazy spectacle
Is what gets the attention
It's not until you have
The perspective of distance,
In the form of time and space,
That allows you to approach
To think about, to process
What happened
And arrive at a better place

January 14, 2018
Galena, Illinois

The phrase, "the perspective of distance" popped into my head the other day and I just ran with it.

Driveway DUI

Sitting on my couch
When I heard a *thump*
Somewhere outside
That sounded like
A car bumping into
A large plastic trash bin
At a relatively low speed
But we live on a busy road
So I didn't really
Pay it much mind at the time
Only that I looked up and saw
The brake lights
From the SUV belonging to
Our across-the-street neighbors
Muted through our curtains
And I figured they hit
Their trash bin. No biggie.
Not two minutes later
My curtains were dancing
With blinking blue lights
From a police car right out front
That's weird, I thought
And paused the movie
I was watching
And opened the door
To see what was going on
And saw three town police cars
And the county sheriff.
Dumbfounded,
I tried to figure out how
My street went from nothing
To being full of police cars
In an almost a too-short amount of time
The across-the-street neighbor guy
Whose name I can't remember
Was standing with an officer
Looking at the front of his car

While the other police
Blocked this stretch of road
Down to a single lane
I went back inside
And started making a batch
Of brownies from a box.
When it was in the oven,
I popped out my side door
And looked around the corner
Of my house to see
The across-the-street neighbor guy
Standing in the road
Brilliantly illuminated
With half a dozen flashlights
Turning his concentrated steps
Into a life-changing production
Fully on stage for all to see
With his performance being judged
By the lighting crew
I went back inside
And watched more of the movie
While the blue lights partied outside
And about the time
I took the brownies out
Was when yellow lights joined in
Signaling the arrival
Of the tow truck
Indicating that he went off-script
And was more improvisational
Than they would have liked
A few minutes later
As he and his SUV
Were hauled away
The road returned to normal
And everything was quiet again
The timer dinged and I got up
To take the brownies out
Just as another car
Zoomed into the driveway

Across the street
The wife slammed her door hard
And police lights returned again
Arriving to tell her what happened
And how they took her husband
For his driveway DUI

Two days later
And I haven't seen
The across-the-street guy
Or his maroon SUV
Just her little white car
Sitting in place all weekend

I undercooked the brownies
But they were still pretty good

> January 14, 2018
> Galena, Illinois

True story. I think he hit something (a parked car? A moving car?) and the police either saw it happen, or someone called them right away. I feel bad not knowing his name, but then again, I've never spoken to him, only his wife once. He and I have nodded at each other once or twice in passing.

Update: The local paper, which lists a very detailed police log for city and county police activities over the previous two weeks, did not mention this incident. Strange.

The Fake Flakes

Outside it's snowing
The fake flakes
That don't seem like snow
Too wide and flat
Too absurdly light
Where it seems like
A mild sneeze
Would easily clear
Half the yard
So I doubt the need
For snowplows
When a leaf blower
Half-assedly duct-taped
To the hood of a car
Would do the trick
Quite nicely

January 14, 2018
Galena, Illinois

A Season Behind

I'm a season behind
With all my scents
As the liquid soap
On the bathroom sink
Smells like autumn mums
But according to the calendar
We're now well past pine

> January 31, 2018
> Galena, Illinois

It's hard to keep current on all your scented products.

The Shining Enticements

The shining enticements
Brightly glittering
Focusing the attention
Up above the chaos
The churning mass
Of daily humanity
Up to a level, a height,
Where the details blur
Into something formless
Into something beautiful
When stepping out of focus
When considering the whole
Instead of the tiniest details
And let the concerns
Evaporate into nothingness

> January 31, 2018
> Galena, Illinois

A few nights ago I was outside and looked up to see all of the stars
in the sky in very crisp detail and the phrase, "the shining
enticements," popped into my head. Tonight I just took the idea
and wrote without thinking.

A Whole Lot Less Interesting

While driving downtown
My eyes glimpsed a bumper sticker
On a car parallel-parked
That said:
"To report erotic driving
 Please call," and listed a number
Which made me do a double take
And after the re-read, I discovered
What it really said
Was a whole lot less interesting

> January 31, 2018
> Galena, Illinois

Sometimes real-life stuff turns out to be disappointing.

Three Phrases Overheard At The Local McDonald's

Three phrases overheard
At the local McDonald's
Which each bothered me
In a sick and a sic way:
"The barn cats decapitate the rabbits,"
"I've got the card because
 I don't trust her with it,"
"Don't worry, she'll ate it"

> January 31, 2018
> Galena, Illinois

Sick. Sick. Sic.
The first one was a farmer guy going into detail on how feral cats
that live in his barn rip the heads off of rabbits for fun without
eating them. The second one was an old couple paying for their
lunch at the counter and the man in the couple said this when the
employee at the register asked for payment. It was one of those
situations where he was trying to make a "you know, *women!*"
joke, which was funny to him and his generation, but comes across
as terrible to anyone else. But, at the same time, I also think he was
being serious. The third one was a young-ish family who didn't
give much thought to proper syntax.

Wedge Of Blue

Each and every time
I ventured outside
Throughout the day
I saw the exact same
Wedge of blue
A clear section of sky
Angled precisely
And consistently
From due west
Triangling up
To the northwest
And sloping down
Terminating north
While the rest of the above
Was a dark and shifting
Mass of thick clouds
Save for that weird wedge
Which defiantly persisted
Despite the chances, the changes
And the surroundings

January 31, 2018
Galena, Illinois

It was weird.

January

Equidistant

FEBRUARY

A Dusting

A dusting
A coating
An even layer
Slightly lightening
Surfaces in the darkness
Quietly tamping
The sounds of the night
Changing the landscape
By absorbing and reflecting
Providing the contrast
Giving the appreciator
A palate for reflection

February 3, 2018
Galena, Illinois

It snowed tonight. Just a dusting.

Falling Out Of Love With A Town

It started simply enough:
Not hashtagging
Photos posted
When twenty, or so,
Used to be normal
My never-mentioned rational
Was that of laziness
Combined with no longer caring

Then it ramped up:
Actively unfollowing
People, tags, businesses, groups
On all forms of social media
Since no one wants to be reminded
Of a past place you'd rather forget
When falling out of love with a town

Because my mind is made up
And squarely focused on the future
Mapped to a different place
More in alignment
With who I am
And who I'm becoming

                    February 5, 2018
                    Galena, Illinois

It's not that I *hate* Galena – on the contrary, it's a very nice town
(to visit). It's just not for us.

You Might As Well Keep Going

It's like seeing someone beautiful
Who has a uniquely specific look
That makes people stop and pause
But after you get to know them
You disappointingly discover
They are vapid, inconsiderate,
And focused solely on the past –
Their own, and your heritage,
Because if your personal lineage
Isn't a branchless family tree
That's been growing right here
For at least several generations
They aren't interested in anything
You possibly could say or suggest
So you might as well keep going
And find a place with inner beauty
That loves you for who you are,
What you bring to the community,
And the greatness achieved together

February 5, 2018
Galena, Illinois

61036

Squirrels Would Make Terrible Cartographers

A fresh blanket of powder-like snow
Giving a canvas-like contrast place
For the tree's shadows to lay down
And slowly spin on throughout the day
Perfect until the fuzzy tails wake up
And scamper all over the pristine scene
With tracks veering and swerving
Like snow prints of drunken college kids
Forcing me to come to the conclusion:
Squirrels would make terrible cartographers

February 5, 2018
Galena, Illinois

Hey, Google Maps, MapQuest (are you still a thing?), Rand McNally, and Garmin, please listen to me. Do not hire squirrels to make your maps. They will be inaccurate.

Sixty Percent Of My Money

I just overheard
Someone say
These two things
In the same single
Conversation:

"I want to spend
 Sixty percent
 Of my money
 On bullshit groceries"

And

"If it's not the bra
 It will be something else"

But maybe, just maybe
I should be a little worried
Because the person
Who said them
Is my wife

> February 5, 2018
> Galena, Illinois

The first quote is probably referring to the dearth of good grocery options in this area, and the second is about something her friend, on the other end of the phone, invented.

Without Alcohol

Being an inadvertent watcher
While my wife takes in
Show after show on Bravo
I have come to the conclusion
After absorbing too much
Of this Housewives network
That they would not
Could not possibly exist
Without alcohol because
The words
The drama
The very fabric
Of every one of their shows
Depends on it

February 22, 2018
Galena, Illinois

Consumed By The Curvature

I stepped out too late
To witness the sunset
But instead I saw
Something better
As the receding light
Had been reduced
To an intense orange ribbon
Threading between
The pigeon blue clouds
And the charcoal hilltops
Its brilliance lasting
Only the width of a whisper
Before it was consumed
By the curvature
And the rotation

February 22, 2018
Galena, Illinois

Stay Safe

"Stay safe"
Is something the teller
Said to us
As we were leaving
Our credit union
On a regular day
Free from bad weather
Or anything else
That might prompt
Such a warning
Making us wonder
If she knew something
We were unaware of
So we ventured out
With a healthy dose
Of caution and paranoia
Just in case

February 22, 2018
Galena, Illinois

When I Pass The Window

Every morning I step down the stairs
And, halfway down, at the landing,
My eyes get a glimpse out the window
And tell me what kind of day I'm looking at
But lately it's been interesting to watch
Over the span of the past week or so
The former solid sheet of deep snow
Thinning into crusty ice
And the deer tracks that punctuated,
Grew, and spread, dappling the surface
Clawing and drawing away
Retreating into the protective shadows
Provided by the garage
The slight ebbing hill
And the thatch of trees
Until tomorrow morning
When I pass the window
And there'll be no snow at all

February 27, 2018
Galena, Illinois

Social Expectations

A person
Small and modest
Spends untold hours
Leaving comments
For contemporaries
Hugely larger and
Much more successful
On Instagram and Facebook
Inserting and interacting
Like it was a full-time job
In hopes for something
A comment or recognition
An emoji, *anything*
All the while thinking
That a response indicates
Acknowledgement, friendship,
Acceptance to their level
So when the meekly modest
Posts something important
The social expectations
Have been set, like a trap
That will never be sprung
As they check back
Every few minutes
Hoping, praying
That the contemporaries
Will comment and reply in-kind
But they never will
Because being a tiny asteroid
Spinning in Jupiter's orbit
Doesn't mean the planet
Is aware or even cares
About imperceptible trivialities

February 27, 2018
Galena, Illinois

After eight months, I still can't type "Galena, Illinois" without messing it up.

Shy Clouds

The availability of clouds
Is a major determinant
Of the quality of sunsets
That we get to see
Not to mention
Their willingness
To participate
In the spectacle
Because shy clouds
Tend to stay out
Of the spotlight
Choosing to put forth
Little to no effort
In showcasing
Their reflective ability

February 27, 2018
Galena, Illinois

Sneaky Sneaky

Sneaky sneaky
Lying in wait
Until the moment
When being pounced upon
Was the one thing
Least expected
By the unsuspecting prey
Who was minding
Their own business
Being peaceful
Until the impending claws
Became airborne

February 27, 2018
Galena, Illinois

The cat stalks the dogs every chance she gets. She doesn't really
"leap" at them on account of her missing a front leg, so she hops
right into their faces and glares.

February

MAY

Currents Unseen

Spirals wrapped around
Tendrils corked within
Eddies churning, riding
Currents unseen but
Steadily carrying on
In an orderly fashion
For a short time
Until the neatness,
Stretched by the distance,
Lost elasticity
And quickly
Dropped all pretense
And descended into chaos

> May 14, 2018
> Whately, Massachusetts

I lit a pinon-wood incense stick when I sat down to write and I could not stop staring at the fascinating double-layered corkscrew patterns the smoke was making.

The Completeness

The hush of winter
The glory of spring
The life of summer
The color of autumn
The completeness and
The beauty of it all

> May 14, 2018
> Whately, Massachusetts

Carefully Curated Catalog Collection

We recently moved
And now we're worried
About the extent
To which our mail is forwarded
Since we want to make sure
We receive our
Carefully curated catalog collection
Because we worked hard
On our junk mail
And we are missing
Our daily mental wealth boost

> May 14, 2018
> Whately, Massachusetts

Seriously…do they not forward catalogs? Blerg. Now we're going to have to re-sign up for all the fancy catalogs again that are full of things we probably won't ever buy, but we love looking at.

Also, I need to note that I have yet to incorrectly type "Whately, Massachusetts," at my normal (very fast) typing speed. Interesting because after nearly a year in Galena, Illinois, I kept wanting to type, "Portland, Oregon" or just misspelling "Galena, Illinois."

I think I'm where I need to be.

Follow The Coincidences

The better I'm aligned
With positivity and happiness
The more frequently I notice
The oddly impossible happenstance
Where things line up too perfectly
Way more so than if left to chance
And I find myself unsurprised
As I follow the coincidences
As the path I find myself on
Widens into a trail of quirks
And speeds into a road
Full of happy accidents
All quickly delivering me
To the inevitable conclusions
I'm making right and left
Quickly coinciding
With the clear and obvious fact
That there is no such thing as coincidence
But rather, they are road signs
Meant to be seen and
Meant to guide us
As we race our way
Through life

> May 14, 2018
> Whately, Massachusetts

Lately, I've been very cognizant of coincidences that are too mind-blowing to be mere "coincidences," so I've been learning to follow them and see where they lead.

A Warm-Weather Blizzard

Snow-white lollipops
Swaying ever so gently
And tilting happily
In the late May breeze
When the wind picked up
And turned the idyllic scene
Into a warm-weather blizzard
Disintegrating and dispersing
The dandelion remnants
As far as the eye could see

May 18, 2018
Williamsburg, Massachusetts

We have a lot of dandelions in the yard. I think we are about to
have a whole lot more in a few weeks.

Will I Go To Heaven?

Recently, I was in line at Target
When a nearby mother warned,
"Don't put that in your mouth.
 It's very dirty."
The small child looked up at her
And excitedly asked,
"Will I go to heaven?"

> May 18, 2018
> Williamsburg, Massachusetts

True story.

The Diction Of Compromise

The diction of compromise
Is most often represented
With cautious muted silence
As history has conclusively shown
This is the safest route
Through most types of trouble

> May 21, 2018
> Montague, Massachusetts

The Heft

Sometimes you need to hold it
To have it right there
The whole damn thing
Firmly in your hands
To fully understand
The weight of the world
To deeply know
The heft it takes
To truly feel
The responsibility
Of having it all
And for those large enough
Who have been impressed upon,
There remains only one
Course of action
And that is to do
Anything you can
To lighten the load
To assist those weighted down
To help in any way possible

May 21, 2018
Montague, Massachusetts

Since the very first time I've meditated, I've always seen myself
gigantic and holding the entire world in my hands while focusing
healing energy on it, and every living thing on it. This one is about
that.

More Shades Of Green

More shades of green
Than you've ever seen
Shadowing above and
Hugging you in
On the curving roads
Right out of a car commercial
To the straightaways
Where the green is
Carpeted out before you
In the fields spread out
Leading to the feet
Of the upsurging hills
Gently rolling along
On their geological scale
Leafy green and perfect
Looking down on the ponds
Reflecting the surrounding color
Directly at you,
Just in case you somehow missed it

                    May 21, 2018
                    Montague, Massachusetts

I grew up in this region, but coming back here after living in the
(comparatively) drab Midwest, the millions shades of green is
striking.

An Exclusionary Mindset

An exclusionary mindset
Seems to be pervasive in
Preventing the residents
From getting too close
To recent transplants
Because they really seem
To only open up to those
Who have roots buried
Five generations deep
If you're any newer
You're only slightly better
Than the tourists tolerated
Only for the money they bring
But this way of thinking
Is working against them
As the younger generation
Moves away to distant cities
And fewer stalwarts remain
In this well-preserved pretty city
Stuck firmly in the past
Refusing to keep up with the times
As it slowly degrades
Into another Midwestern ghost town

May 21, 2018
Montague, Massachusetts

I read that the state of Illinois is working to make a by-pass of
Galena on Route 20.

An Antiquated Throwback

The tinny-speakered melody
Loudly squawking its churned tune
From an approaching ice cream truck
Used to be a child's siren's song
Like a tuna can being opened
Magnetically yanking any cat
Within earshot to your feet
But now
It means nothing to modern kids
It is an antiquated throwback
To the days when children
Would actually go outside
Today, they rarely have a need,
Or are even allowed,
To venture outside

> May 21, 2018
> Montague, Massachusetts

Crave The Disconnect

Something pre-basic and primal
About being part of a non-thinking
Constantly moving, dancing
Human mass of people
With the music louder than yelling
The bass pounding through chests
No time for philosophizing
Arms up, eyes closed,
Mouth open in pure joy
Writhing with the wall of flesh
To the songs without end
Blending into one another
Just like the revelers
As the lights flash
Rhythmically, hypnotically
Combining to form
A sensory overload
To those who crave the disconnect
And want to plug into something
Bigger, greater, than themselves
For a few glorious hours of freedom

May 26, 2018
Whately, Massachusetts

We just watched the Netflix move, *Ibiza*, which has several scenes at clubs like this. I've never been to a rave myself (do they even call them "raves" anymore? I dunno.) but the closest I've come to it was when I saw Bjork in 2002, she had a couple of her fast "clubby" songs that melted into one another, and with the lights, the sound, and the crowd going nuts, it really felt like it.

Trying To Remember

Trying to remember
The great idea I had
That I came up with
Just yesterday
But sadly, sitting here
Under the ornate tin ceiling
Of the busy café
With the sound and smell
Of jaunty piano music
Swirling together in concert
With the thick layering
Of freshly ground coffee
Punctuated by the occasional
Clattering of plates
And the steady background
Droning of scattered conversation
Inside
While I look out the window
At the passing traffic on Route 9
And the billowy greens
Of the maple trees across the street
Swaying in the breezy late-day winds
Looking picture-perfect
With the help of the low-lying sun
Brightly-lit light green
Contrasting nicely
With the shadowy side of each branch
Deeply-dark emerald
And all of a sudden
I realize I don't care
About what I've forgotten
Since I've gotten
So much more
From my minutes
Of being lost in thought

May 30, 2018

May

Hadley, Massachusetts

Real Estate Size-Up

The other day we went to an open house
From the pictures, it looked pretty nice
But not a place we would actually consider
But it did have nice elements that we may
Want to consider sometime in the future
But for now, we showed up and looked
With the dozen, or so, other lookers
And in every nook we ended up going
Where there were other people
They visibly checked the two of us out
Like some kind of real estate size-up
Where they determined their chances
Of getting the house if it came down
To them versus us in a bidding war
In some instances I caught a quick smirk
Other times they averted their eyes
Maybe out of shame at having been caught
But either way, each and every couple
We came across did the same size up
For this house we really didn't want
Which I inwardly found to be funny

> May 30, 2018
> Hadley, Massachusetts

We went to two open houses and it happened at both places.
Weird!

May

Equidistant

JUNE

Hills Upon Hills

Hills upon hills
Stacked up beyond comfort
To a beautiful extent
In an area
Where the nature
Is stunning
But the town
It surrounds
Is depressing
Nestled in this place of extremes
Happiness up high
With sadness below
Makes me want to appreciate it
From a safe distance
Reducing the ramshackle
To a collection of tiny steeples
Above a speck-like semblance
A crumbling collection
Of empty buildings
In this forgettable town
While magnifying the magnificence
Of the mountains towering around

June 8, 2018
North Adams, Massachusetts

I think North Adams has improved since I was last here but it still feels depressed. It's a weird juxtaposition with the fancy, highbrow Mass MoCA modern art museum and boutique restaurants and inns contrasted with the empty storefronts and run-down houses. Hopefully it will continue to improve.

Dipped A Toe

Dipped a toe
In the emerald hat
Of the Berkshires
But did no more
Than circumnavigate
The interior of the brim

June 11, 2018
Montague, Massachusetts

Before we went to North Adams last week, the phrase "Dipped a
toe in the hat of the Berkshires" popped into my head.

Emotions Now Inverted

The sad sad day
When my paintings
That haven't sold
Need to come down
Each time I reach up
I grab another work
I hung a month ago
Filled with potential
As I reminisce about
The stories behind
Each and every one,
The hours of work,
And my happiness
When I hung them up
Emotions now inverted
As I take them down,
Wipe the dust off,
And unceremoniously
Load them in my car
Hoping that someday
They'll find a home
And be appreciated

June 11, 2018
Montague, Massachusetts

While writing at the Western Massachusetts Writer's Meetup, I watched an older woman come in and take down her art that was hanging on the walls. That got me thinking about what it feels to be that person who has to take down their art feeling like no one wants to buy their work.

Saleable Potential

Thank goodness
Today's the day
When the old art
That hasn't sold
Gets taken down
Blanking the walls
Making room for
Something new
Hopefully with
Saleable potential

June 11, 2018
Montague, Massachusetts

This one is a continuation of the last one ("Emotions Now Inverted") but from the perspective of the café owner.

The Top Leaf

The top leaf
Of the tree
Is the leading edge
Standing tall
Gathering energy
Helping to advance
The limbs below
While down
Deep underground
The lowest root
Stretches out
Gathering water
And nutrients
For the trunk above
And these systems
Seemingly independent
Work together in tandem
For the good of all

> June 20, 2018
> Northampton, Massachusetts

While driving yesterday, the portion of the road I was on bridged over another road and I was up high enough to be eye-level with a nearby tree. I saw the top leaf and was struck on how the tree itself is an interesting representation of society in general.

A Quick Stop

Staring up at the night sky
Asking for help from
Someone, anyone up there
Who has been through this
And can easily step in
And put a quick stop
To the terrible troubles
We're currently mired in

June 20, 2018
Northampton, Massachusetts

Seriously, why can't those aliens* just land already and help us out?

*Benevolent, non-invading aliens only, please.

Repeating

The idiots who put us here
Clearly either never bothered
To learn history
Or skipped it entirely
Because we seem to be stuck
On the treadmill of stupidity
Repeating mistake after mistake
We should have easily avoided
So we find ourselves hitting
Every single pothole
Each one deeper,
Each one doing
More damage than the last
And we're now at the point
Where we're going to need
To pull over and call for help
And get a tow…
But who will come to our aid
When we've littered the Internet
With such scathing, hateful reviews
Of anyone who could possibly help
So with all of our bridges burnt
And with nowhere to go
We'll be stranded
As a result of our own ignorance

> June 20, 2018
> Northampton, Massachusetts

It is absolutely sickening to witness what's been allowed.

Astonishingly Congruent

The complexities of
The concept which
Binds everything
Is exceedingly simple
And astonishingly
Congruent with
The neat and tidy
Orderly existence
That's expected
With natural systems
Evidenced from
Scientific observations

June 20, 2018
Northampton, Massachusetts

I don't know what it means. Sorry.

Gives Me The Gift

Sometimes knowing the answers
To the biggest questions in life
Make the normal day-to-day stuff
Seem incredibly inconsequential
And gives me the gift
Of complete freedom
From want or worry
From fear or stress
And puts me at such ease
Allowing me to appreciate
Existence from a place
Of complete joyousness

June 20, 2018
Northampton, Massachusetts

Sometimes Life Won't Let You

No matter how much
You may want it
Despite all the times tried
Sometimes life won't let you
Forget
Leave
Walk away
From the things
That once held sway
The things of towering importance
To someone who didn't know better
So many lifetimes ago
And, one way or another,
Like a boomerang
Or migratory birds
You find yourself there
Or it returns
Either way
You need to face it
Once again
Every time
Until you've learned the lesson
That life's trying to teach you
So keep going back
To face it head-on
And understand
You can get past this
And move on
To the next lesson

June 30, 2018
Whately, Massachusetts

A no-thinking, just writing kind of poem while listening to
"Disintegration" by The Cure.

It Looks Pretty Outside

It looks pretty outside
On an overly sunny day
Until you make the mistake
Of opening the door
And the blast of heat
Slams you like a dry wave
That leaves you drenched
Before you can reach the car
Where your second mistake
Stings worse than the sun
Stabbing your squinting eyes
As the ovenous interior
Bakes you like burnt toast
Before you can manage
To get the windows open
But it doesn't help that much
Because it's nearly 100 out
And you shouldn't have
Even considered leaving
The comfort of the house

June 30, 2018
Whately, Massachusetts

It's been a beautiful spring, and now the full fires of heck have been focused on the region.)=

Delete The Voicemail

When the memories of your past self
Inevitably decides to give you a ring
In the telephone of your mind
Do your present self a big favor
Don't answer it
Delete the voicemail
And forget it even happened
Because the past can never not try
To delay, to ensnare, to bring you back
In an attempt to keep itself alive forever
Don't let it
Let your future achievements be your destiny
Not the long-forgotten events of your past

June 30, 2018
Whately, Massachusetts

JULY

The Cat Led Me Down The Hall

The cat led me down the hall
Meowing frantically
Like Lassie leading rescuers
To the well where Timmy was
But much more desperate
She has used this method before
To inform me of catastrophe –
Her bowl of chow being empty
So I learned to be aware
Of her when she communicates
So I hurriedly followed
As she trotted quickly
Turning frequently to see,
And ensure, I was still behind
Then, after much commotion,
She flopped down, flipped over,
And licked her butt

July 1, 2018
Whately, Massachusetts

True story.

Why Can't I Be An Artist

Why can't I be an artist
The kind that gets written about
In places like the *New Yorker*
Or featured in modern art museums
The kind who put out work
Indistinguishable from that of a child
Or at least someone in high school
Who paints something sloppy
Whose photographs are blurry
Whose music lacks melody
Who writes prose chaotically
And are absolutely showered with
Praise, kudos, acclaim, and
Profound, flowery descriptions
Worthy of a true masterpiece
That had deeply impacted
And changed the very fabric,
The very consciousness,
Of our culture and civilization

July 1, 2018
Whately, Massachusetts

Modern art, for me, falls into one of three categories:
1. What the hell am I looking at?
2. I could totally do that.
3. That is mind-blowingly amazing.

The thing I have a hard time getting over is when someone will write a huge article about a piece of art as if it were the savior of the universe, and it's just something like a torn piece of paper with an exceptionally crude drawing of a house that's been stomped on with a dirty boot.

The Car Who Would Not Move

The light ahead turned red
So I pulled up to the line
And waited at the busy intersection
Thirty seconds later
With the light still red
The green Prius behind me
Driven by the late 50s
Or early 60s man
With multiple passengers
Honked impatiently at me
Spooked, I looked up
And verified the light's redness
Then I glanced in my rearview
To see the man peevishly
Toss his hands up as if to say,
"What the hell! Move!"
But the light was still red
And my destination was ahead
So I sat there and watched
As the cross traffic streamed by
Another aggravated beep
From the Prius' owner
Whom, I'm assuming
Wanted to turn right
But didn't want to wait
For the light to turn green
And there wasn't any room
To attempt to scoot on by
I don't know what he wanted
I couldn't pull ahead
Through the red light
For I would surely be
Broadsided by traffic
And I wasn't going to turn right
To accommodate his wishes
Since I wanted to go straight
So I brushed off his brusqueness

July

And waited patiently for the light
I believe he honked a third time
But I told myself to ignore him
Like I ignore the comment sections
In any and all online news websites
When the light finally turned green
I pulled forward very normally
While I heard his little tires screeching
As he tore around the corner
No doubt scaring his passengers
With his irrational rage
At the car who would not move

July 4, 2018
Whately, Massachusetts

This happened earlier this evening around 7:30pm in Northampton
at the intersection of King Street and Damon Road. It was so
weird. I mean, what did this guy want me to do, roll into traffic
through a red light, and get hit because he wanted to turn right?

Today Is Independence Day

Today is Independence Day
Today we did something different
Instead of participating in
The typical American ritual
Instead of doing the required
Grilling and blowing shit up
We went downtown
To the courthouse lawn
To the annual ceremony
So we could cheer on
And add our clapping
To that of the hundreds
Who had also gathered
To welcome,
To support
The several dozen immigrants
Who were granted US citizenship,
Something we take for granted,
But they know the true value of
They, the future of our country

July 4, 2018
Whately, Massachusetts

A few days ago when I read about this citizenship ceremony, it just felt like the right thing to do; that we need to show immigrants that they are wanted and needed here.

Squash Cukes

It never fails
At this time of the year
As June rounds into July
And the heat seems to increase
From the *Simmer*
To the *Boil* setting
The signs are everywhere
"Squash Cukes"
Which I can only assume
Is either some sort of protest
Inciting people to rise up
And destroy cucumbers
Or
A local sportsball team
Will soon be athleting against
The dreaded "Cukes"
Playing out another chapter
Of their deep-seated rivalry
Either way, I don't get it

> July 8, 2018
> Whately, Massachusetts

To be fair, some of the signs say, "Cukes Squash."

Because That's How This Nature Thing Works

Lately, the weather has been
More traditionally moderate
Instead of the increasingly hellish heat
We've been progressively accustomed to
And I would like to accept the credit
For the thankfully cooler temperatures
Ever since I've taken to lighting
Earthy, autumn-scented candles
Because that's how this nature thing works

                July 12, 2018
                Whately, Massachusetts

You're welcome.

The Momentum Of Existence

Sometimes you don't get a chance
To pause and rest
Even to just take it all in
Sometimes life just goes too fast
And if you halt, even for a moment
You could get rolled over
By the momentum of existence
So, push yourself and keep going
Because once you stop
You may not get started again
And if you need a breather
Do it after the big stuff is done –
I guarantee you the view
Will be a whole lot better

> July 12, 2018
> Whately, Massachusetts

My mother is buying a home and is a bit frazzled by the whole process as she keeps saying she feels like too much is coming at her too quickly. As I told her, soon it will be over and she will be a lot happier in her new place.

You Can Tell The Tourists

You can tell the tourists
By how they look
By how they act
By how they hold themselves
Soft, out-of-place, doe-eyed,
Unguarded and unaware
Making them an easy target
From a full block away
I want to avoid
Looking like them
So I steel my face
Projecting no-nonsense
Letting slip no emotion
Staring straight ahead
While walking with the purpose
Of being somewhere else
Sometime soon, so I walk fast
But I still steal glances
I can't help it
Surrounded by so many
Towering buildings
Interesting architecture
And the busyness
Under it all
I still look up
But carefully
So as to not be detected
Or marked as an outsider
Who doesn't belong

July 20, 2018
New York, New York

I went to the city to see Dramarama play at a little club in the
Village. Whenever I'm in a big city, I'm always afraid of being

targeted by a pickpocket, robber, or any nefarious person like that, so I do what I can to minimize that impression.

Meant To Be Hidden

On a train you get to see
All the things
That are meant to be hidden
From the public-facing view:

The colorful swirls of graffiti
Mostly terrible, but here and there,
You see something beautiful,
Funny, or downright astounding –
Museum-quality and inspiring

The junk cars, long dead,
Rusting in backyards
Without hope or a chance
For some kind of resurrection
Or repurposing through recycling
Just a quiet reclamation by nature

The industrial refuse
They refuse to dispose of properly
Because that isn't profitable
So there it sits, in great big heaps
From now until long after
They go out of business
And it eventually becomes
"Someone else's problem"

The forgotten empty factories
Abandoned and overgrown
The windows' angrily sharpened snarls
Carefully crafted by teenagers
Using thrown rocks like paintbrushes
To leave their mark in sculpting the building
While their brethren tag reachable surfaces
Indicating this is theirs

You see these things

July

And a whole lot more
The kind of things
You normally don't see
Because that contrast
To your normal life
Is what sparks thought
And hopefully action

July 21, 2018
Whately, Massachusetts

Interesting things seen from the train.

The Wind Wasn't Refreshing

The wind wasn't refreshing
Cool, energizing, reviving,
Like I expected, like I wanted,
Instead it blew hard and hot
Ahead of the approaching storm
Gusting an angry warning
Telling me in the only way
It had to communicate
To me, to everyone around,
To go – to get inside now
Because things are ready
To get more than a little bumpy
When the stronger section
Makes its appearance soon
Accompanied by the rain
Much heavier, much harder,
Than you're comfortable with
So I heeded the threatening wind
And hustled back inside
Where I watched the darkness
Roll in
Where I felt the thunder
Shake through
Where I saw the deluge
Pound down

July 23, 2018
Montague, Massachusetts

The Old American Dream

The old American Dream
Was a simple one
Where you'd get married,
Have a few kids,
Get a good job
You'd work until you retired
And own a house
With a week-long vacation
Thrown in there every year
And this would be life
At least that's how it seemed
When I was young

Now –
Those who came before us
Are trying to deny people
Who are in love
From getting married
And barring them
From having kids,
While the rest of us
Aren't becoming parents
Or, are at least delaying it,
Because we can't afford it,
Meanwhile the notion
Of having a single job
And keeping it for life
Is like something
From a fairy tale,
A true impossibility
In our world today,
Vacations happen
But are much shorter
And might instead be
A long weekend
Somewhere nearby,
While owning a home

Is completely unlikely
With costs upwards of
Seven figures, and rising,
This dream I was taught
Has been pushed beyond
Any normal person's reach,

And I have long arms

> July 24, 2018
> Whately, Massachusetts

I almost never write in the morning, but when I got up I had the idea for this and the next poem so I immediately sat down and wrote them.

The New American Dream

Everyone knows what the previous generations
Taught us about "The American Dream:"
Owning a house, having kids, a good job for life,
Yearly week-long vacations, and retiring happy
And for a long time, that's all people wanted
Now the very notion seems quaint,
Like an unreachable, antiquated fairy tale,
Because the times have changed and we live in
A nightmare dystopian future from some bad movie
And, for the majority of us, The Dream has changed.
The New American Dream is not based
On materialism but instead is much simpler:

Don't shoot me.

> July 24, 2018
> Whately, Massachusetts

When children in every school in the entire country practice drills
on what to do when an "active shooter" is there, and no one feels
safe, The Dream changes.

Peak Summer

We're steeped deep in summer
And everything around me
Seems to indicate it'll never end
But still I'm spending time
Looking for the subtle signs
Trying to figure out when
We've reached peak summer
When the billion green trees
Start to dull ever so slightly
When the bounty of vegetables
Found at all the local farm stands
Start thinning in quantity and quality
When the Halloween candy
Appears in the supermarkets
And the *Back To School!* signs
Show up in the big box stores
When the sun sets a little earlier
And gets a little more noticeable
Each night, night after night
Until you start thinking about
How much daylight you've lost
All of the signs and all of the things
I've been noticing are telling me
That we're right in the midst of
Peak summer and if I'm not careful
It'll be completely over
And I'll have missed it entirely
As the season folds into fall

July 28, 2018
Whately, Massachusetts

A Hot Dog On A Hot Day

There he is, a hot dog on a hot day
My dachshund walking in the yard
With a slow-purposeful gait
I've seen before
And I watch intently
As he slows down
Lengthening his steps
As his long body
Gets closer to the ground
The blades of grass
Parting before him
Looking like an oil tanker
Through the ocean
Until he stretches out
Past the point of no return
Stops walking, tips over,
Lying fully elongated
Soaking up as much sun
As his lengthy body can absorb

> July 28, 2018
> Whately, Massachusetts

This was Baxter today.

AUGUST

The S Apostrophe Removed

I noticed the fancy wooden sign
That once proudly stood watch
In front of the neighbor's house
With their name carved so nicely
Within a swirl of embellishments
Got changed with a single rough cut.
On my way to work, it was one way
On my way home, it was another
And now the meaning has been altered
With only the S apostrophe removed
Implying that things on the inside
Have changed permanently

August 8, 2018
Hadley, Massachusetts

That S apostrophe carried a whole lot of weight.

Reinvention

At one age
It seems as if life is going
Firmly in a certain direction
And you head that way
Chugging along at full speed
But then
Things change
Sharply
And after a time set adrift
In a place that's unfamiliar
And completely unknown
From where you thought
From where you planned on being
Stunned, wondering what happened
Some people in this place
Break down completely
Pining away for the life
They feel is due to them
They feel should be theirs
Some people though
Go through a period
Of introspection
And experience
A type of reinvention
Where they pick themselves up
And rebuild their lives
With what they've been given
With what they have in-hand
And are surprised to see
They are now in a better place
Than they would have been
Before the life-altering change

August 8, 2018
Hadley, Massachusetts

Bad Seat

I inadvertently chose
A bad seat at the café
As my back is facing
Those waiting in line
And one by one they
Are all reading what
I'm writing, reading
This poem right here

August 8, 2018
Hadley, Massachusetts

Yes. I wrote this about you.

Pet The Cat

Always be sure
To pet the cat
With the grain
Or they may
Return the favor
By petting your arm
Deeply, with claws,
In the same manner
That you may not like

August 8, 2018
Hadley, Massachusetts

Slicing Saturn

Standing here boots-deep
On Dione's rocky surface
Mostly featureless, except for the view
Oh, that exquisite view
Which brought me here
And is keeping me standing
Appreciating this vantage
Of seeing the rings
As if they were
The blade of a sword
Edge-on, swinging at me
So sharp, so thin
Slicing Saturn cleanly in half
With only the hooped shadow
Betraying the angle
Of how hugely wide
They radiate outward
From the looming giant
Pastel-banded background
Dominating everything
In this corner of the system
And, without turning,
I watch the small inner moons
Swing around, spin, and dance,
Their shadows painting dark dots
Tracing along the planet's surface
And if I turn slightly I can see
The hazy copper hue of Titan's orb
Doted with the lights of civilization
One of which, calls to me as home
But for the moment, I am here
Enjoying this view that I never tired of

August 8, 2018
Hadley, Massachusetts

In my weekly writer's group I go to, we always say who we are
and what we're working on (for the benefit of new members).
When I say I'm working on my next poetry collection and my next
sci-fi novel, someone inevitably asks if I write science fiction
poetry. I always thought this was kind of a dumb question, I mean,
who writes sci-fi poetry? Who's even heard of such a thing? Well,
I looked into it and it definitely is a thing, so I figured I would try
my hand at it. This is my first sci-fi poem. I think I will be writing
a lot more.

The Epicenter Of Remembrances

When the beats start
I quickly realize I am near
The actual physical place
The epicenter of remembrances
That make this song
So powerful in my mind
Correct in geography
But off by decades
Which works to distort
The effect of the memories
And the impact is lessened
Due to the quality
Of my current life
But had I been in a different place,
Emotionally,
Each note would have been amplified
Each word sung would have stung
The effects would have been magnified
Like a catastrophic earthquake
Shaking my very soul
Down to the foundations
And then pulverizing them
Into the ground
Without mercy
Without regard
To the person I had become

August 8, 2018
Hadley, Massachusetts

Not the case at all, but I was thinking how music can really affect some people.

The Grounding Pull

When your life consists of
Nothing but gray and black
And a distinct lack of gravity
You begin to truly long for
The vivid greens and blues
And the grounding pull
From a place, a home
You've only seen in pictures

August 11, 2018
Whately, Massachusetts

Another science fiction poem about someone born elsewhere in the
solar system, most likely on a moon, or an asteroid, and wanting
desperately to go to Earth.

Getting Myself Out There

Getting myself out there
Is something I've never considered
Is something I've never done
Is something I always thought was a waste of time
I mean, why spend time doing promotion
When I could use that time actually writing
So, for years I stayed far away
Spending my creative time
In my own poetry bubble
Happily writing and building
That year's poetry collection
Then I moved here
And began to meet
With other writers
And saw that every single one of them
Is solely focused on promotion
On getting their stuff out there
And I saw people
Whose work is ok
But they have recognition
And the publishing credits
Associated with someone
Of a much higher stature
All because they kept
Submitting, submitting,
Submitting, submitting,
Constantly, every week,
Every thing they ever wrote
Thrown against the writer's wall
Like spaghetti
Just to see what sticks
And here and there
Something did stick
Now that publishing credit
Is prominently featured
In their bio on their website
Which is otherwise empty

I look at my body of work
Which is considerable
But I am passed over,
Overlooked for my lack
Of credits in magazines
And literary journals
Despite the ten books
I've written over the years
Which seem to mean nothing
To these other authors
So here I am
Getting myself out there
Going crazy submitting
Sending my work far and wide
Starting at the top
And staying there
Because I know my worth
And I won't submit
Just to adhere
To lowered expectations

> August 11, 2018
> Whately, Massachusetts

Joining my writer's group has been a huge eye-opener for me. Seeing how focused everyone is on "getting published," seeing other people being very full of themselves because they had a poem published in a magazine, etc, has really made me very motivated in getting out there. I know I'm good, but it does nothing for me if no one knows who I am or if my books are not read. I'm changing all of that and have submitted a bunch of poems in this collection to some of the most respectable magazines. I guess my changed mindset has worked already – Garrison Keillor re-read my poem "Riding The Red Line" (from *Anything But Dreams*) on his show, *The Writer's Almanac* this past week. The last time he read that poem was in 2011. Let's hope my work finds the right outlets to be featured in.

Update: I submitted poems to one contest and five magazines and journals. I'm still waiting to hear back from two of them, but nothing accepted yet. Am I worried or concerned? No way. I'll submit a few more this year, and every year thereafter. At some point something will get accepted. Until then, I'll keep writing like I have been.

This Museum Was Just A Dream

The dream was crazy vivid
With details so extraordinary
Which found me in a museum
I've never seen before
And most likely exists nowhere
But in my own mind
With art so beautiful
In a building so striking
Whose curves and crannies
Should be studied by students
From every corner of the world
And I was in this museum
Playing the online game
I enjoy every night
But this felt really real
With me on the blue team
Guarding, protecting this building
From the inevitable onslaught
That the red team was planning
So I walked around with my guns
Looking for the best places
To defend from invasion
But I kept getting distracted
And staring at everything
Because this place was so amazing
With details so breathtaking
That several times I stopped
Pulled my phone out of my pocket
And took photographs
Of the Instagram-worthy scenes
Like the marble statue
Bathed in the ideally-soft
Late afternoon light
Streaming in from
A nearby oversized window
While behind the statue
Was another huge window

That overlooked a flower garden
Bursting with blooms
Providing an idyllic backdrop
Also covered with that perfect light
I spent what felt like hours
Making my way around
Planning strategy but also
Appreciating the beauty
But I woke up before
The mission even started
And my first inclination
Was to reach for my phone
Filled with the excitement
Of possibility of posting
These insanely ideal photographs
And my joy turned to confusion
At not seeing the pictures
Anywhere on my phone
Then I woke up more
And realized this museum
Was just a dream
And so were my photos

August 15, 2018
Whately, Massachusetts

When I have a few hundred million dollars lying around, I'm totally building that museum. That, and pay someone to make a playable map of it for Team Fortress 2.

Self-Imposed Literary Roadblocks

At a fiction writer's Meetup group
For the first time, to check it out,
I found myself sitting across the table
From a man who had the most
Bizarre questions about writing:
Asking what is the modern definition
Of the "Great American Novel"
Saying he was stalled and confounded
Because he wanted to write it
But had no idea what it was now;
Asking how successful we were at inserting
"Post-post modernism" into our books
Because he saw a movie once
Which he felt was in that style
And assumed everyone who wrote
Now tried to emulate that in their writings;
Asking how many books we read a year
He was astounded by all of our answers
Saying that he personally hated to read
And couldn't imagine reading anything
Which made me stop and wonder
What was he doing here?
And how was it possible
That he was even writing a book?
Listening to him dominate the conversation
Over the span of two arduous hours
Where each thing out of his mouth
Was more ridiculous than the last
It was like he was someone
Who had heard phrases somewhere
That were just beyond his grasp
And he felt like it must mean something
Important, so very important,
So he tried to apply them to his book
Finding the round pegs not fitting
Into the square holes he had before him
And was getting frustrated by his own

Self-imposed literary roadblocks
So we gave him advice
(So much advice)
And hopefully set him on a simpler course
Telling him to forget everything
That's stopping him
And to just write

August 15, 2018
Whately, Massachusetts

Holy hell, that was a very frustrating Meetup.

Every Monday night I go to my writer's group called Protagonists And Procrastinators where we meet at the café by the Montague Bookmill (which has the best slogan ever of, "Books You Don't Need In A Place You Can't Find"). At that Meetup, we spend half an hour just talking about stuff before we put our headphones on and jump into writing for a solid hour. That talk time before (and after) writing has been hugely beneficial and helpful to me, and everyone who attends. We have the best discussions about writing and publishing.

On Meetup.com, I saw a different writing group that meets at the Uno's at the Holyoke Mall once a month. They don't do any writing at the meeting, but instead it's a three-hour discussion about writing and publishing for fiction writers. I thought it sounded great so I went last night. Yikes-a-rooni. One guy there dominated 95% of the discussion by saying the most random stuff and asking such weird questions. I don't think I'll be returning. I didn't get anything from the meeting, and I've been on a carb-free, sugar-free diet for the past two months and Uno's is probably one of the very worst places for me to try and find something good to eat.

A Barrier Between

Time is a separator
A barrier between
Us here in the now –
Distancing us along
From what we were,
With no regard given
As to whether or not
We had completed
What we intended –
Pulling us towards
What we will become
Again, indifferent
As to our preparedness

> August 16, 2018
> Whately, Massachusetts

I think one of my biggest issues with existence in this life is time. In my day-to-day life, I'm always on-time and it's not an issue (in fact, being at the right place at the right time is one of my secret superpowers). My problem with time is its acceleration the older I get.

Sailing Right On By The Exit

Driving along the Interstate
Humming along at a good clip
But clearly not paying attention
Sailing right on by the exit,
Where there was someplace
I knew about, thought was cool,
And really wanted to visit,
It's no one's fault but mine
Since it was clearly marked,
But I wasn't paying attention
So, oblivious to the signs,
I completely missed going there
Which I didn't even notice
Until days on down the road
I stopped to rest and realized
I stupidly missed my chance
To experience something
Genuinely neat and unique
And now I was too far away
To just turn around and go back
So I have to push onward
On my cross-country trip
Knowing I missed my chance
And hopefully, at some point,
I will be able to get back there
And finally see it for myself

August 16, 2018
Whately, Massachusetts

This has happened so many times in my various moves and cross-country drives. One that really sticks with me is I really wanted to go to Rock City. For hundreds of miles going down towards Georgia, while on my move to Alabama, I saw the "See Rock City" signs. When I lived in Alabama, I always meant to go there, but never made the time. When I moved back to Massachusetts, I had driven by the exit and not even realized it until somewhere in Maryland. I've really gotta learn to pay more attention to the signs and stop to smell the roses when they present themselves.

The Time For Reflection

I've heard
Them say
The time for reflection
Is not now
But when
You have nothing else
Better to do
With life

August 16, 2018
Whately, Massachusetts

I have a soft spot for the poems that follow a shape. In this case, it's eight lines where the top half reflects the bottom half.

Blinding Myself

Blinding myself to the news
Of the world, of the day,
Setting aside the insanity
Leaving it for others
To dissect and comprehend
Giving me a needed breather

> August 16, 2018
> Whately, Massachusetts

This is really short and weird, but I like it. Especially how the lines begin: gerund, non-gerund, gerund, gerund, non-gerund, gerund. It feels like a longer haiku or something.

The Exact Same Thing

Knowing what I know now
Would have changed things
Considerably back then
But life happens the way it does
For a reason, I mean, it must
Otherwise we wouldn't be here
But instead be somewhere else,
Wondering the exact same thing
About a different situation
And where the untaken road
Would have delivered me to

> August 17, 2018
> Whately, Massachusetts

Holy hell, do you have any idea how many carbs popcorn has?
Geez! I would eat popcorn for dinner (often!). I sometimes wonder
how thin I'd be if I was more aware of the bulking effect that carbs
and sugar has.

Emotional Crowbar

Wanting to write
Something very
Light and fluffy
As airy as candy
Sweet like toffee
But, sadly, nothing
Seems to be coming
To mind that'll fit
Maybe I'm not
In the right mindset
Maybe I'm trying
Too much, too hard
To force happiness
Amid all this sadness
And finding that the
Emotional shoehorn
Isn't big enough to do
This big job properly
Which is why it is
A good thing I have
An emotional crowbar
Because I'm determined
To make this work
One way or another

> August 19, 2018
> Whately, Massachusetts

My last few poems haven't been the most cheery, and I like to switch things up as I write, so I wanted to write something happy and light...*but* nothing came to mind.

Now It's Normal

At one time we were really smart
It wasn't long ago, but things have changed
Now it's normal for people to be
Constantly questioning the facts
Despite knowing they are solid
Dumping pure faith into speculation
Or, worse yet, into things easily disproven
Thinking this must be the right way
Because this is the road we're now on
In the dumpster rolling down the hill
Unfathomably fast, on fire, smoke billowing,
While everyone else watches and wonders
How we got from where we were
To the dire predicament we're in now
And how to ensure it doesn't happen to them

August 20, 2018
Montague, Massachusetts

I Cheated

An obsession has been
Knocking around my head
For weeks and months now
It was all I could think about
Day-in, and day-out
How the scene would unfold
Played and replayed
Over and over, again and again
I couldn't hold back any longer
Lured by the curves I craved
I drove over there
I came right out
Made my intentions clear
And said what I wanted
They were happy to oblige
And so very quickly
I had what I wanted
So hot in front of me
And without a further thought
I dove in headfirst
And I cheated
On my diet

August 30, 2018
Whately, Massachusetts

UGH! In the two months I've been on the keto diet, I've lost 36
pounds. That's awesome. *But*, I've been really craving
McDonald's hard. For pretty much the past 20 years, I've eaten
there at least once a week, usually twice. Tonight I went there.
Was it good? Kind of. The fries were good. The burger was good.
The soda tasted watery and like chemicals. Was it worth it? No. No
it wasn't. And now the heaviness of the carb/sugar load in my
stomach feels like cement. Now all I can think of is to wonder how
far this indiscretion will set me back in my weight loss. Ugh.

Equidistant

SEPTEMBER

The Tree In The Side Yard

The tree in the side yard
Is one of two things:
It could be intently aware
Of what is to come
So it is acting first
As an autumnal prophet
By shutting off the chlorophyll
Turning on the color
And dropping leaves
Hoping to signal
To anyone paying attention
That a seasonal change
Is looming on the horizon
Or
It's lazy.
It punched out,
And is just done
With 2018

> September 1, 2018
> Whately, Massachusetts

Me too, tree. Me too.

The Lid Was Missing

I opened the door
To the refrigerator
And sitting right there
On the second shelf
Was a plastic container
The kind of thing
That supermarkets use
For anything store-made
This container held
Shredded parmesan cheese
But the lid was missing
Which made me wonder
Why the heck would my wife
Put it back in the fridge
Without the covering to it
I went to pick it up
So I could put plastic wrap
Or something to cover it
And quickly discovered
As my finger bounced off
Some unseen surface
That it did, in fact, have a lid
But it was unusually clear
So perfectly unblemished
That it was completely invisible
Like it was not even there
No reflection, no nothing
To indicate a lid was present
Causing this exact scenario
To replay four separate times
As I repeated my actions again
Hours later in the evening
And when I mentioned this
To my wife, she said
The same thing happened to her
Twice as well
Causing me to mark it

With a Sharpie
So we don't get fooled
By the oddly tricky lid

> September 1, 2018
> Whately, Massachusetts

True story!

Two Magnets

Acting like
Two magnets
Pulling
Crossing
The distance
Deliberately placed
Between them
Like some kind
Of cosmic magic
Ignoring reason
Ignoring warnings
Pulling
Despite intention
Unaware of the power
Each actually holds
Nothing like a magnet
Instead, more like
Two neutron stars
Spinning
Orbiting
Around, toward
One another
In a spiral
Not wanting
Ineffectively avoiding
The eventual
Collision
Which will
Inevitably
Destroy everything

Whately, Massachusetts
September 1, 2018

Have you seen computer simulations of what two neutron stars colliding look like? It's fascinating, and that type of star collision is responsible for nearly all of the heavier elements in the universe.

The Obligations Of Death

When the wife becomes the widow
People you know just show up
Every day for weeks on end
Every one of them –
From deeply concerned neighbors
Who have known you for years,
To looky-lou acquaintances
That travel in the same social circles
Who just want the inside scoop –
Every one of them
Wants to know
How it happened
How you're holding up
If you need anything
So you tell the story
Over and over
Re-live the horror
Over and over
Tearing you up inside
Again and again
So you lie and say you're okay
Over and over
Each repetition
Makes you want to scream
Over and over
The obligations of death
To re-live, to repeat
To be there for them
Making them feel better
About themselves
For being there for you
The obligations of death
Hold you to a societal standard
You give zero fucks about
When all you want
When all you need
Is space

And time
To grieve
To deal with it
In your own way

When the wife becomes the widow
You don't get what you most need
You don't feel like you can be normal again
Not while everyone is watching
Not while everyone is studying you
Not while everyone is discussing you
Even if you've dealt with the passing
And come to terms about the departure
The abruptness of it, and the drastic change
It means for you in the short term, and in the long term
You have to hold in any feelings
That aren't utter emptiness and sadness
Which you still feel, of course,
But we're complex creatures
Capable of so much emotion
The confliction crowding
Filling our heads and our hearts
So many different directions
So many different feelings
All at the same time
Two weeks after the fact and you don't dare
To let slip a laugh at a cat video
Appearing in your Instagram feed
Or some other kind of silly nonsense
Just in case someone might overhear
The happy noise coming from you
And glare at you, narrow eyes
Silently condemning,
For not acting, for not playing the part
Of the still suffering widow
Which you are, no question about it,
Which is why you still feel the need
To remain vigilant and guarded
With all emotions, with all expressions

September

Because no one will understand
That even though he died
You're here, and still very much alive
And for you and your children
Life still continues on
Yes, much slower now,
With more reflection
On the fragility of existence,
But it moves on nonetheless

September 2, 2018
Whately, Massachusetts

Recently, a friend's husband passed away. From observing everything that happened, I came to realize there are too many societal expectations burdened upon the widowed. I know everyone *means* well, but we all deal with death differently and the survivors do not need the additional stress of the obligations we put on them (whether real, or [rightly] imagined).

Each New September

This weekend we are
Sheltering in place
Avoiding the hordes
The massive throngs
Of swarming students
Tens of thousands
Returning to school
At the area colleges
Filling, clogging, causing
Parking lot-like roads
Endless lines at stores
Filling the police blotter
With drunken exploits
And eroding our faith
In humanity a little more
With each new September

September 2, 2018
Whately, Massachusetts

Geez, it's not nearly that bad! I sometimes tend to exaggerate. The students are great. They keep this area fresh and interesting.

Cleaving Existence

Try as we might
Want to wish
That everything
Everyday be bright,
Sunny, and cheery
With no negative
Anything anywhere
But merely considering
A world without contrast
Is violence upon reality
By removing exactly half
Of the equation
Of what we see
Of everything
Cleaving existence
Like Thanos but with
Darker intentions
By people who want
To only see the part
That agrees with them
And nothing else
Forgetting that we need
Disparity and difference
Which enriches everything
From what we see
To what we experience
And all that lies between

September 10, 2018
Whately, Massachusetts

I was looking on Submittable and saw a call for submissions for a literary journal where the subject was (essentially) "darkness." I opened Word and gave it a go. I don't think I succeeded in writing something I can submit for that magazine, but I like it enough to include in my collection.

I was also secretly pleased to be able to work in that Thanos mention so easily.

Keep Myself Normal

The moonless night
Is deceivingly quiet
Considering the constant
Screaming, echoing
In my mind, in my head
But the words don't
Ever find their way out
Instead they stick tight and smell
Like freshly spread hot asphalt
The kind you're not sure
If it's safe to drive on
But you still do anyway
Because others are doing it
And you've got somewhere to be
But the burnt hardness scent
Stays with you miles beyond
You ever would have expected
Which is how I feel right now
With my thoughts contained
Stuck in the oval enclosure
Responsible for confining
My consciousness during this life
But it feels like I received
One, which is the wrong size
One, which is much too small
And the pressure of the thoughts
Multiplying exponentially
Day in and day out
Year after year
The energy building
Is threatening to burst
Unless by working
I can try to keep up
And keep myself normal
Like I appear
On the outside

September 10, 2018
Whately, Massachusetts

Trying another "dark" poem. I actually have a playlist I created in my iTunes called "Dark," so I listened to that while writing from the point of view of someone who's got some issues. I think I was fairly successful (more so than the last poem), but I don't think I'll submit this one either.

Sunflower Tree

We've reached the part of summer
That borders the warmest edge of fall
Where the huge-faced sunflowers
Have all settled down for their annual nap
But the little sunflowers are fully awake
Watching over the pumpkin patches
In their always happy, dancing way
Which describes the scene today
When I was driving and saw
Something oddly incredible:
What resembled a sunflower tree
A single stalk, which branched out
Fifteen or twenty times up its frame
Each one ending with a cheery face
All facing different directions
Unlike the nearby field of sunflowers
Looking like something someone made
Who had way too much time, glue,
And 50% off coupons at Michaels
But was actually, amazingly real
And planted right there in the ground
For us to enjoy for this short time
As we drive past on our way home

> September 10, 2018
> Whately, Massachusetts

I don't know if "big" sunflowers grow at different times than the "little" sunflowers, but it sure seems like it.

But yeah, that sunflower tree is nuts! I've never seen anything like it before.

A Repeated Vision

There's a repeated vision
I see of myself
And have seen
For many years now
Taking place sometime in the future
It's just me
Standing in a house
A very modern house
A very expensive-looking house
Standing in the open space
Between the huge kitchen
Open off to my left
And the beautifully appointed
Living room to my right
The only light
Is flickering from the gas fireplace
Expansively wide and illuminating
The thick repurposed-wood coffee table
And the very long, very nice leather sofa
The back of which,
My right thigh is leaning on
I'm aware of the kitchen's existence
With a huge poured-concrete island
In the periphery on my left
But I don't look there
My future self's mind
Seems to be deep in thought
Of what? I have no idea
But my passing attention
Lazily rotates between the fireplace,
The drink in my hand,
And the floor-to-ceiling window-door ahead
The flickering light sliding across, through, and around
The diminishing ice cubes
In the copper-colored liquid
Monopolizes my focus first
Then a long stare into the fire

September

Followed by my eyes being pulled
To the post-twilight near-darkness
Through the view out beyond
The very wide and deep porch
Which, while I'm unable to see
Due to the navy-to-black sky
I know it overlooks an ocean
Or some equally impressive,
Equally eternal, body of water
Where, during the day,
One's attention would be captured
By the perfect horizontal line
Representing something bigger,
Something beyond what we are
But, in my vision, it's not the day
It's nearly night and I have a feeling
That this scene is important
I don't know why
I don't know how old I am
I don't know where my wife is
I don't know where my pets are
I don't know where this is
I don't know how I afforded it
I can only assume it's my house
Because I seem to feel at home
But I also know I am alone
Maybe I'm celebrating something
But have no one to share the news with
Maybe it's just a normal night
Or perhaps it's my last night with this life
Or maybe it's none of these
I have no idea because
I can never see before or after this
I only get this several second scene
Every once in a while
Which only leaves me with more questions
Each time it makes a surprise appearance
In my mind
During dreams, out shopping, or while meditating

All I know is that it is me
And it's the future
That's it

September 10, 2018
Whately, Massachusetts

My Eyes Are Rich

My eyes are rich
With the view
Glorious beauty
Everywhere I look
Layers upon layers
Surrounding me
Enticing, tempting,
Asking, appealing me
To keep appreciating
To keep taking it all in,
As if I weren't already
Dangerously in love
With this whole area
Until the very end

> September 14, 2018
> Whately, Massachusetts

Today in the car we were about to go over the bridge between
South Deerfield and Sunderland, Massachusetts when Kari looked
at the fogged-topped hills all around us and said, "My eyes are
rich."

Everywhere And Everywhen

I am everywhere
And everywhen
In every place
Every time
Every life
Stretching back
Looking forward
I am all of those
All at once
Right now

September 20, 2018
Whately, Massachusetts

Time is not linear.

I Want That Knowing

While living this life
Starting right now,
Going forward,
I want that knowing
Whispering all the time
Giving me the solution
The gut feeling
That's always, *always* right
Telling me the answer
To everything
Shining like a neon sign
Cutting through the dark
Anytime I'm speculating
About anything
I'm not left wondering
I just *know*

September 20, 2018
Whately, Massachusetts

I've been really interested in those kind of people who live their lives not by rational decisions, but by what their gut says. I want to be more like that.

Every day I meditate. This is kind of dumb, but after each meditation session, I give it a grade. Most days are in the B-range (like, "today was pretty good, it was a B+"). Today my meditation was a solid A+. I haven't had one like that in a very long time. For probably a solid hour after the meditation was over, I was feeling residual "effects" from it. This included feeling like I was full of energy, and an unusual (for me) connection to my higher self. Every time I thought about anything, I just *knew* the answer. It was really cool. It was during this time, when I was outside walking the dogs, I had the general idea for this poem. As I was writing it, I got caught up with the notion that I needed to put a word ending in "-ing" in every line. I thought it make it rhyme and flow in an interesting way, but then realized I was getting too caught up in trying to make it fit so exactly when is when I stepped outside of that box I had put myself in.

So Dark So Early

So dark
So early
So used
To light
So late
I'm not sure
I like this
Darkness
Or where
It's going
But there's
No way
To say
"Stop it!"
And have
The Earth
Listen
To me
And make
It right
To fix
The night
Because
The Earth
Does what
It wants
Which is
Darkness
So early

September 20, 2018
Whately, Massachusetts

It's 7:30pm and it's fully dark? Geez. Stupid Earth and its darned axial tilt.

I spent an embarrassingly long time writing and editing this one. I like it because it's something a little different from what and how I normally write.

What I also like about this poem is that this is a topic I write about every year and I often get a little worried about how I am going to comment about the same annual events but in a different way. I think I succeeded.

Nature And Man Conspired To Censor

A small-town arts walk
Set in a field
Leading into the woods
Where poetry will be read
Inspired by the sculptures
Standing watch over the trails
At the very first stop
As the first poem is being read
The honking flock swoops in
Slowly, at first,
Then becoming distracting
Before finally too loud,
Overpowering the poet's voice
For a painfully solid minute
As the large flock passed on by
Overhead to somewhere nearby
Everyone laughed
But the moment was marred,
Her poem forgotten,
Interrupted by the birds
A short walk found us at the next stop
Where the next poet began to read
Until a few lines in
When the small plane
Followed the flock's lead
With its engine *rrrrrr*-ing loudly
Eventually overshadowing
The verses completely
For another awkward minute
And by the time it had passed
The poem was done
As we walked to the third stop
I thought how both
Nature and man
Conspired to censor
The poetry
Almost as if they knew

What we were in for
And worked together
To lend their voices
And thoughts to enhance the piece

September 25, 2018
Whately, Massachusetts

On Sunday I went to an Arts Walk at a nature preserve in Southborough, Massachusetts. The art was good here and there, and so was the poetry. I thought it was funny that right off the bat, a flock of geese disrupted the first poem being read. Then, at the second art stop along the trail, a plane flew overhead. I sometimes like to imagine unrelated events (flock of geese and the plane) are actually completely related in a strange cosmic way.

As a side-note, I wish "Southborough" were spelled, "Southboro."

As a note stemming off of the side-note, if we did that we would probably have to spell, "dough" as "dō," and that would be weird.

Poking That Bear

Poking that bear
Sitting over there
Not bothering anyone
Just doing bear stuff
Like looking for honey
Or whatever they do
Is probably not smart
But it would get views
On my YouTube channel
No ten-foot pole needed
I'll use my fingers
Just like God gave me
Because, again,
That would be better
And get more shares
Setting the bar
A little out of reach
So tomorrow
And every day thereafter
I'll need to come up
With something superior
And completely unexpected
Until I retire or die

September 25, 2018
Whately, Massachusetts

Just thinking about how YouTube content creators must feel at
having to continuously grind out videos every day that are more
interesting or shocking than the last one.

The Then And Gone

The more I live in the present
The here and now
The more that the past
The then and gone
Fades away
And becomes forgotten

September 25, 2018
Whately, Massachusetts

The Things That Mattered

The things that mattered
SO MUCH,
The things that were
SO IMPORTANT,
Back then,
So long ago,
Are the things
That are dulled down,
Faded, and
Mutedly bleached
Until they are left unrecognizable
With the unkind and uncaring
Passage of time

> September 25, 2018
> Whately, Massachusetts

I still had the theme of the previous poem in my head when I wrote this one.

Salmon To Peach

Salmon to peach
To orange to neon
Completely and utterly
Not noticed by and ignored
By the other occupants
Of this car who were busy
Talking about something
What, I don't know
Because I was floored
As the entire evening sky
Horizon to horizon
South to North
Was set ablaze
Swaddled and bathed
In vivid, luscious colors
The likes of which
I had never seen
And I will never forget

September 25, 2018
Whately, Massachusetts

My friend and her mother were in the front seat talking about people they knew or something but I was staring, dumbfounded, at the brilliant color and the incredible width of the stunning sunset. It was amazing.

Eventually, they did comment on how beautiful it was. But, at the time, I was thinking, "How are you not seeing this?"

Walking On Eggshells

Years and years experience
Of walking on eggshells
Has given me the conclusion
That the shells themselves
Are getting thinner every year
Making it much more likely
That I'll stumble on my walk
Leaving me to apologize
For making bigger messes
Repeatedly and consistently
Despite my working harder
To be much more cognizant
And aware of when the shell
Is starting to crack, to prevent
My feet from stomping through
Leaving nothing other than
The ruined remains of untold
Mashed eggs all over the road
And me feeling like the remains
Are splattered all over my face

September 26, 2018
Whately, Massachusetts

I love scrambled eggs!

A New Version Is Needed

Forty years ago
The Cure had a song
Called "In Between Days"
Which now seems outdated
Since we no longer have
The patience or the time
For anything resembling that
So a new version is needed;
Something along the lines
Of, "In Between Seconds,"
Or, "In Between Jiffies"
Which, sadly,
Doesn't sound right

September 26, 2018
Whately, Massachusetts

I don't know why, but "In Between Jiffies" really cracks me up.

September

Equidistant

OCTOBER

I Misread A Flyer

Today I misread a flyer
Which I thought was for
The Cigarette Arts Festival
Which seemed strange
Considering the location
And the state in question
Until the double take told me
About the Garlic Arts Festival
Which seemed more appealing

October 1, 2018
Whately, Massachusetts

I could see a Cigarette Arts Festival happening in the Carolinas, but not in Massachusetts, despite the fact that this area is lousy with tobacco barns.

All It Takes Is A Month To Change Your Beliefs

All it takes is a month
To change your beliefs
That ninety degrees is hot
To eighty degrees is hot
And seventy is starting
To feel unseasonably warm
But this is where we find ourselves
Riding the downward wave
From light late to dark early
From too hot, to nice,
To bundle-up cold
But we're not there yet
As we're sitting squarely
In the middle of "nice"
With the deep heat
Thankfully forgotten
And the frosty frigidity
In the oblivious future
Way too far from now
To even think of caring about

October 1, 2018
Whately, Massachusetts

Late To Its Own Funeral

We've already forgotten October
Whose calendar ends tomorrow
Standing here
Facing the shadow of November
Looming large over everything
Wondering where
The normality of the seasons went
As I watch the foliage erupting
Beautiful colors everywhere
Picture-perfect scenes happening now
Instead of three weeks ago
When it should have peaked
Making the autumnal season
Late to its own funeral
Delaying the inevitable
Oversaturated pictures
Posted by the millions
All over Instagram

October 30, 2018
Whately, Massachusetts

It makes sense on a warming planet that the cooler seasons would be delayed.

AllOneWord

A newer word that we all say often
But is never really recognized
Is alloneword
But seen typed out seems weird
Because it's only spoken
And only in reference
To directing someone
To something seen
On a computer

October 30, 2018
Whately, Massachusetts

Although, it seems that companies who market products and
services are constantly jamming two words together ("try our
brand new PeopleChow!"); probably because it's easier to register
a trademark that way or something.

Trapped In A Purgatorial Place

In this candle company's call center
Is a collection of transitional people
Trapped in a purgatorial place
Where they all spend their stints
Making a barely passable amount
While looking for something better
In the rare times when they're not here,
Getting yelled at by old people
Who can't figure out how use
The discount code on the website
Where there is never not a discount
And never not a shortage of people
Looking for meaning and fulfillment
In an autumn-scented candle

                    October 30, 2018
                    South Deerfield, Massachusetts

Almost

The cubicle assigned to me this evening
Was standard in its sparseness
With a computer monitor,
A phone, and some papers
Tacked to the fabric walls
With codes and numbers
Needed for reference to do the job
The one tiny detail
That made this one different
From all of the others
Was the torn top of a Post-It
Stuck over the bottom right corner
Covering three-quarters of an inch
Which was just enough to block
Window's little pervasive clock
And on it was written the word:
Almost
With a little smiley face
Which completely made my day

October 30, 2018
South Deerfield, Massachusetts

When I was in the Boy Scouts, and I was going for my Vigil
Honor I had to stay up all night long, keeping a fire going while it
was raining. That night I learned the importance of not looking at
my watch to help the time go by faster. The kind soul who left this
torn corner of a Post-It note over the clock on this computer also
knows, and I thank them for the wonderful reminder.

The Noise

The Noise
Starting low
Rumbling up
Deeply ominously
Reverberating shaking
Rising quaking
Like the fear
Making everyone
Running fleeing
Until surpassing
The simplest expectations
Of realistic survivability
When there's nowhere to go
And nothing left to do
Other than stand firm
Appreciate everything up to now
And turn to face the end, head-on

October 31, 2018
Whately, Massachusetts

I was listening to K. Flay's song, "Blood In The Cut" when I head the word "noise." I figured since it was Halloween, I would write a little something to fit in with the theme of the day.

All The People

Sometimes when I'm out in public
In a big box store or a supermarket
I notice all the people around me
Each and every one busy carrying on
With their own lives
Working on their life goals
Learning their life lessons
Dealing with their own stuff
Each and every one with a reason
For being here, on this world,
At this time, doing this same thing,
Existing,
Just like me

        October 31, 2018
        Whately, Massachusetts

Except for dressing up on Halloween. That is not like me at all.

Backup

I'm doing something now
But I have a backup fully in place
And am working on another
Backup of the backup
Which is the route I would prefer
And very likely to traverse
In the end when I say goodbye
And sorry to the first thing
And the backup, both of which
Are actually counting on me
But I need to look out for myself
And what's best for my interests
Because I can't treat myself right
If I allow others to ignore
The best parts of who I am

          October 31, 2018
          Whately, Massachusetts

Jobs!

This Autumnal Season

This autumnal season has been
A nearly futile exercise of
Endless driving and searching,
Looking around and seeing
Occasional pinpoints of beauty
On an otherwise drab canvas
Carefully wrapped tight and hidden deeply
Locked in a basemented storage room
In an unvisited, overlooked museum
Sentenced to an ignored small city
In a neglectedly flown-over state
None of which has managed
To garner a single positive review
On any app, website, or social media platform

> October 31, 2018
> Whately, Massachusetts

Having grown up here, I expected MUCH more of fall in New England.

NOVEMBER

Equidistant

It has recently come to my attention
That my next birthday puts me
In the awkward equidistant place
Of middle, middle age
Midway between thirty and sixty
Falling precisely between
The fading twilight of youth
And the official start of being "old"
And I don't know how I feel about it.
What I do feel is that I am
Too far gone to go to clubs
And enjoy the indie bands
Whose music I like so much
With crowds half my age
But I'm still too far away
For age-specific condos
And early-bird specials.
I am most likely past
The halfway point
Of my life expectancy
Considering my lifetime
Of eating nothing but
High-carb, high-sugar foods,
And the lack of exercise,
Or regular doctor visits,
One would expect or assume
But we're not here to discuss
My eventual mortality
Which is a subject I'm calmly,
And rationally, at peace with,
But rather the matter of this
Middle-middle point
I've progressed into
Which has taken the form of
A scenic vista point
Where I am offered
A sweeping picturesque outlook

Of the valley of my life.
What's ahead is uncertain
As the road continues
Beyond where I can see,
Up and around the bend,
But it's nearly impossible
To resist pulling over,
To stop and enjoy the view
Of what I've done
And where I've been
But I can't stay long
And I need to be cautious
Because this is the place
I've heard too many stories about
Where the act of lingering
Can cause pangs of longing
For the various nouns
Left, one way or another,
Firmly behind in the past
Now visible, right down there
Which I could see clearer
If I put a quarter in the
Pay-per-view binoculars
To bring it closer, so close,
Seemingly separated only by distance
But no one ever figures on time,
The greatest of all separators,
Completely uncrossable
In the way we want
Until the realization hits
And deepens into crisis
Which is why this parking lot
Is full of abandoned cars
From others before me
Who arrived at this very place,
Looked out over the view,
Saw something they liked better
Than where they were heading,
And leapt off the edge

Only to eventually crash and burn –
Chasing something extraordinary
That had existed for a brief time
But was no more anymore;
Like an unreachable memory
Damned and determined
To claim another soul
At the bottom of the bluff.
So, I am happy that I am cognizant
And level-headed enough
Not to go jumping off the cliff in crisis
Instead being thankful for
The various wonderful experiences
I have been fortunate enough to have
While still appreciating the journey,
And the anticipation,
Of where I am heading
Despite not knowing
How this whole thing
Will end up turning out

November 7, 2018
Whately, Massachusetts

When I first came up with the idea for this poem, I had planned on saving it for my 45th birthday next year, which would be the true equidistant point between 30 and 60. However, I also thought, "That's silly. Why not just write it now instead of saving it for five months."

Mildly interesting note: For nearly the entire year, I had been planning on calling this poetry collection, *You Might As Well Keep Going* because I thought it encapsulated the feelings of living in these really messed up, turbulent times; then I came up with *Equidistant* and I really liked the simpler feeling of it compared to the "well, you're going though some shitty stuff, so keep going to get to the good stuff,"-feel of the previously planned title.

Yesterday Flew By

Just as yesterday flew by
So shall today
And everyday thereafter
Forever and ever

November 22, 2018
Whately, Massachusetts

I feel obligated to follow one of the longest poems I've ever written with one of the shortest ones. There's a symmetry with the balance of things in there somewhere.

Putting The Lunch Before The Holiday

Over the past week, I've been guilty of
Putting the lunch before the holiday
Because my work handed out free turkeys
So I cooked it up and turned it into meals
That I've been reheating every day
Like some kind of an advance showing
Diminishing the desire for the real thing
Ensuring I get tired of the main course
Days before the actual celebrated day

November 22, 2018
Whately, Massachusetts

My favorite meal is Thanksgiving dinner, so I was really excited
when my work handed out free turkeys to everyone. Now that the
actual holiday is here, I'm not so crazy about having a full-on
turkey dinner anymore.

The Bridge

The bridge
Between me and you
The most essential
Piece of infrastructure
Containing only
The most important
Freely flowing ideas
And contemplative discourse;
The things that sustain us
And make life and time
Worth so incredibly much

November 22, 2018
Whately, Massachusetts

Late At Night

Late at night
With the darkness
Surrounding, shrouding
Everything
And I'm inside
Locked in tight
And going nowhere
Until the morning
When the day resets
To something new
And I am free to go
And once again
Experience
The potential
That life has to offer

November 22, 2018
Whately, Massachusetts

It sounds neat and noble and all of that, but how often do we truly say to ourselves, "Gosh! I'm going to do that thing I've always wanted to do today!" and actually do it? Not often enough. Take advantage of the potential a new day offers.

Now That The Meal Is Over

Now that the meal is over
We charge straight on into
The next holiday, sitting off
Over there, a month away
The decorations are all up
The lights are shining here,
There, and just everywhere
Despite feeling tired, we go
And won't stop until it's done

November 22, 2018
Whately, Massachusetts

Ugh. So full…but the Christmas lights are so pretty.

Quickly Strung

I'm now inside, shivering with pride
From the twenty minutes outside
Where I hung the Christmas lights
Quickly stung in a half-assed fashion
Adhering to our cultural tradition
Which, thankfully, is now happily,
Wholly, and completely customary

November 25, 2018
Whately, Massachusetts

True story!

Present Imbalance

Every year there is
Almost always
A present imbalance
Between me
And just about
Everybody
It's not that I don't care
Because I definitely do
It's just that it always
Slips my mind
Combined with time
Which always seems to
Slip out of my grasp
Pretty much guaranteeing
That I'll always feel awkward
When someone gives me a gift
And I'm left with nothing
To hand them in return

> November 25, 2018
> Whately, Massachusetts

Sorry in advance! Actually, this year we were *really* good about Christmas cards; we sent out a batch of 50-something cards on Friday.

Tricky Indeed

I know why I'm here
I know what I'm supposed to do
But I don't know why
The things I know will happen
Are taking so long
Except that it must be
Part of a life-lesson
I'm supposed to be learning
But don't have the patience for,
Or, it could be something else
That I'm not aware of
Which would be tricky indeed
And unsurprisingly par for the course
In this oddly complicated universe

November 25, 2018
Whately, Massachusetts

In The Quiet Space

I've reached an age
That sits comfortably
In the quiet space between
Weddings and funerals
Where the last of our friends
Are having the last of their kids
So we're out of major life events
Until aunts, uncles, and parents
Decide they've had enough
And start to check out
Till then, we'll spend our time
Enjoying and appreciating
What we've got while they're here

> November 29, 2018
> Whately, Massachusetts

Is It About Me?

"Is it about me?"
She asks nearly nightly
From the living room,
While I'm writing poetry
At the computer in the office
"Did you write about me?"

Tonight I can reply, "Yes, I did."

November 29, 2018
Whately, Massachusetts

Staring Down His Driveway

I don't know why
But the other night
I had an odd thought
Just pop into my head
Someone who I haven't
Given any thoughts about
For at least thirty years
But there he was, in my brain
My neighbor's father,
Younger then than I am now.
What I acutely remember,
Despite the decades of distance
The ashey stank of Pall Malls
That statically clung to him
Like a too-tight sweater
Releasing that striking,
Face-wrinkling,
Stale cigarette smell
Everywhere he went
But he never got much further
Than the garage
Where he hung out
With the double wide door open
And the mostly empty cooler's
Top was propped up
While the Natty Light empties
From that day's session
Were lined along neat rows
In the cardboard tray
About to join the other
Several dozen cases
Stacked against the back wall
Waiting for his monthly trip
To the recycling center
But there he was
Standing there
A cigarette in one hand

A beer in the other
Aviator sunglasses
Perched low on his nose
Under the undefined shape of hair
That didn't match any known style
Which had gone fully white
A generation too early
Just staring down his driveway
Staring and thinking
In his favorite way

November 29, 2018
Whately, Massachusetts

I don't know why I thought about him. Weird.

November

Equidistant

DECEMBER

Most Awards

It doesn't matter what
But most awards,
For some unknown reason,
Lack the ability, the empathy,
And open-mindedness
To even remotely consider
Anything light, fun, or funny
It all has to be gut-wrenchingly
Sad, severe, dramatic, and stagey
The kind of thing most of us avoid
Because that's now our normal life
But if, in your chosen creative field,
Your work doesn't bum you out
Or repeatedly reduce you to tears
It's not worth any sort of award
Or officially sanctioned recognition

> December 8, 2018
> Whately, Massachusetts

Seriously, why is this the case?

When The Outside Better Matches The Words

I had several ideas
And more than a few lines
Of poetry written
That I wanted to shape
And bend into something
To celebrate this time of year
But unfortunately
They were meant for autumn
They've been sitting, waiting,
A little too long
And now it doesn't feel right
Despite being only a few weeks old
The season isn't quite right
Doesn't really match up
To how things are now
So I'll set them aside
And hopefully
Find a use for them
Next year
When the outside
Better matches
The words

December 8, 2018
Whately, Massachusetts

In all actuality, I'll probably totally forget about these idea
fragments.

Despite The Emphasis

Sometimes it's hard
To get motivated
To get moving
To get doing
The things you know
You should be getting done
Not just because
You have to
Or you want to
But because
It's your Purpose
It's the Reason
You're here
On this planet
At this moment
In this body
In this location
All things you *know*
But still
Despite the capital letters
Despite the emphasis
The drive and the momentum
Can be as hard to catch
As trying to start a fire
By lighting soaked wood
With a single, broken match

December 8, 2018
Whately, Massachusetts

The List Of My Superpowers

The list of my superpowers
Is small but well-documented
And undeniably impressive
In a world where such things
Are fully reserved for fiction
And not for average people
Living normal lives today

First and foremost
I have an uncanny ability
To always, always, be
At the right place
At the right time
Despite the traffic
And the best intentions
Of life to get in the way
I still find myself
Where I need to be
At the exactly right moment
I mostly squander this power
With taking photographs,
Getting ideal parking spaces,
Or catching green lights

Also, I can control clouds
I know this sounds weird
Since clouds are always
Moving, shaping, changing
On their own anyway
Without input from anyone
But it's something I can do
On overly overcast days
I'll tear a hole in the blanket
Letting me see a welcome patch
Of blue sky in the sea of gray
Oh, last night is a good example
We were at a stargazing event

And the guide was explaining
How to find the constellations
When I saw a solid wall of clouds
Approaching ever so slowly
At first covering a quarter
And then a third of the sky
Threatening to ruin our plans
Of looking through the telescopes
At the stars and planets above
So, I concentrated, focused,
And simply erased the clouds
With my mind, I reached up
And just wiped them away
Dispersing them evenly,
Quickly, and completely
Saving the night for us
And the three-dozen others
Who had come to see the stars

Another is my ability
To spark my creativity
Anytime, upon demand
Like how I sat down
A few minutes ago
With nothing planned
Not knowing what to write
Only that I wanted to
And I've knocked out
Four poems fairly fast
I can't even comprehend
Writer's block because
The ideas flow faster
Than I have the ability
To write them all down
Like I'm standing there
On a tiny, rocking boat,
Holding a pint glass up
As I float over to the base
Of a crazy Niagara Falls

December

Where the unfathomable
Torrent of water is ideas
More than I could ever
Hope to capture, re-tell
Or do something with
But, for me, it's always
There, always flowing
With so much inspiration
In a deluge of thought
That'll never go dry

None of these translates
Or even begins to compare
With what the superheroes
Can do on the big screen
But for an average person
Doing average things
It feels pretty extraordinary

December 8, 2018
Whately, Massachusetts

My Sink Does This Thing

My sink does this thing
When I turn it on
To an average flow
Yes, the water goes
Out the faucet
In the regular way
But it also leaks out
Somewhere between
The faucet body
And the escutcheon
Pooling slightly around
The back of the sink
Until some of it drains
Down and out the drain
While I clean up the rest.
This issue never happens
When I've got the sink
On full-blast, or a trickle,
Only when it's set on a
Normal amount of water
I know it's something
As stupidly simple as
Replacing a faulty O-ring
But instead of fixing the issue
I make myself go all or nothing
Each and every time I reach
For one of the most basic
And critically needed elements
To continue my existence.
Is my faucet trying to tell me
I should change my pace
And always be going
All-out! All the time!
Or is it trying to convince me
The opposite is true…
That I should learn
To live in the moment

December

And savor the slow life.
Or, or, or,
I'm spending too much time
Thinking about silly things
And I should just fix it
So I can do my dishes
Without having to worry about
Water spilling out everywhere.

December 9, 2018
Whately, Massachusetts

While doing the dishes tonight I was thinking about how this faucet was acting as a metaphor for life and getting absurdly too-thinky into that notion. While writing this, I realized the answer is simple: fix it. Done.

A Quick Review

Appreciated my youth
Timided my teens
Enjoyed my twenties
Squandered my thirties
Re-examining my forties

> December 16, 2018
> Whately, Massachusetts

I had a happy childhood. I was a big introvert in my teenage years. I had an enjoyable run in my twenties. I spent most of my thirties working tons of hours. Now, that I'm in my forties, I'm looking over my life and figuring out how to live a fuller, happier life that more mirrors my hopes and dreams.

The Ultimate In Contrast

Recently I have found myself
Living the ultimate in contrast
Spending my days
Working a governmental job
Looking at forms,
Counting up numbers,
Stamping papers,
Writing my initials
Sending them onward
To other people
Who will do similar things
With no variation
With little real thought
With no room for creativeness
Of any kind whatsoever
Day in and day out
For the foreseeable future
While the nights are filled
With buckets of imagination
In the form of innovative expression
Writing, painting, theorizing, doing
Creatively constructing something
Fun, new, vibrant, and enjoyable
Filling my soul with the bright life
I know I was meant to be living
Which will hopefully completely
Outshine and leave far behind
What currently occupies my daytime

December 16, 2018
Whately, Massachusetts

It's really frustrating doing something that doesn't allow me to
utilize any of my knowledge, experience, abilities, or passions.

You Don't Yawn In Your Sleep

You don't yawn in your sleep
Unless you're not in deep
Enough to know or to show
That you're really asleep

December 16, 2018
Whately, Massachusetts

Weird and simple. I wrote down the first line in my notes yesterday and ran in a very rhymey direction.

All Those Long-Gone Months

I can't seem to avoid it,
The signs are everywhere
No matter where I look
Directing my mind back
To a very specific time
I have moved away from
In a firm and deliberate way
As if the Universe was
Trying to tell me there's
Something unfinished
Back there I need to deal with
But I choose to ignore
Those frequent reminders
Because the past had its chance
Before being buried completely
By heaps of pages torn from
All those long-gone months
Multiplied by so many years
Forming sedimentary layers
Over the subject in my heart

December 16, 2018
Whately, Massachusetts

Protocol And Paperwork

"How is that a 'me' problem?"
Asked the person working
In the government position
To someone who dared
To offend by not being aware
Of which form to use when lost
In the endless and confusing maze
Of protocol and paperwork

       December 16, 2018
       Whately, Massachusetts

New Traditions Through Technology

In the past we had so many things
We could count on that gave us comfort
That we no longer really have
Which is why we've since developed
New traditions through technology
Don't have a fireplace? No problem.
Just fire up Netflix
And watch one of a dozen hour-long
Programs that just shows a close-up
Of a fireplace burning and crackling
Pick your favorite type of wood
And turn your giant 4K ultra high-def screen
Into the never-had fireplace of your dreams
Want to listen to Christmas songs 24/7
But don't own a radio
That's outside of your car?
We've got it covered
Turn on Spotify or Pandora
And stream those sleigh bell songs
Non-stop for weeks on end
Sick of fighting crowds in stores?
There's no need to go there anymore
Just go to Amazon.com
And order everything you need
For everyone on your list
And it'll all arrive in two days
With no shipping charges
Not even Santa can beat that

December 22, 2018
Whately, Massachusetts

All It Takes Is An Instant

All it takes is an instant
The briefest of moments
Where the faint, but there,
Whiff of alcohol
On your boss's breath
As he passes by
In the hallway
Changes your opinion
And your impression
From that second onward

December 22, 2018
Whately, Massachusetts

So Much Energy

The feeling of being filled
So overflowing with
So much energy
From meditating
Is something I want to feel
Every day, all the time
From now on, until the end
Filling, emanating, radiating
Just being a normal part of me
Like the hot hands that heal
And the intuition guiding
Me so perfectly through life
Always landing exactly
Where I need to be
When I need to be there
The perfect-fitting part
Filling the ideal space
And I couldn't be more
Thankful and appreciative
To the Universe
For orchestrating it all
So everything ends up
Better than expected
Time and time again

December 22, 2018
Whately, Massachusetts

I meditate every day and have done so for the past year now. When I'm done, I secretly grade my meditations based on how it went. If I spent the entire time with muddled, random, and excessively distracted thoughts, I'll think, "That was a D." Most days, I tend to average a B. Sometimes a B-, other times, a B+. Today, I had a solid A+ meditation. It was like *WOW*. It was so powerful that I still felt out of it (in a good way) two hours later.

More, please!

Spanning The Tapering Months

The nightening of the scenery
The diminishing of the season
Spanning the tapering months
From life-green vibrancy
To rusty, leather-like dying
To bare-branch nostalgia
Remembering back,
And looking forward,
To the time when
The world blooms again

December 22, 2018
Whately, Massachusetts

We Are Hapless

Despite our attempts
To constantly resist
We are hapless
To the wantings
Of the soul

December 23, 2018
Whately, Massachusetts

It's All Planned Out

In my mind, it's all planned out
The ebbs, the flows, the edges,
The cover, the interior, all of it
It's there waiting to be released
For the fingers to do their work
Despite this, the idea of ditching
The work in progress is so very
Appealing, stopping everything
Abandoning the idea, & starting
Something brand new entirely
Something fresh and unplanned
Just heading in a new direction
And not stop until I arrive there

> December 23, 2018
> Whately, Massachusetts

This sounds completely bonkers, but despite being in the middle of writing my next novel, I'm considering shelving it and going in a completely new path. What? Why? I don't know yet. I've been tossing around the idea of challenging myself to writing one short story a month and at the end of the year, I'll have a collection ready to publish. Either that or write a book on spirituality. I know those are radically different directions, but that's where my gut is leading me.

You should *always* trust your gut.

Also, when I was writing this poem, the surprisingly consistent widths of each line was somewhat of a happy accident.

The Same Complex Coin

The dreamlike ethereal
Like a projection of life
Playing across clouds
Both here, both real,
Two sides of existence
On the same complex coin

December 24, 2018
Whately, Massachusetts

Speaking In Similes

Speaking in similes
Because the mental image
Better conveys the point
Than a hundred words
Which is helpful when
Your mind is so completely cluttered
With absolutely no room to move around
Without repeatedly bumping into things
Like the crazy-stacked attic of a hoarder
Discovered by relatives after they died
But, to them, the layout and placement
Made perfect sense, and everything there
Had a deliberate purpose and a reason
But, an outsider, unfamiliar with the "why"
Would dismiss it all and order a dumpster
Tossing treasures and incredible things
Ignorant to the real riches they were faced with

        December 24, 2018
        Whately, Massachusetts

I was intending on writing about how my mind always seems like such a jumbled mess of neat and interesting things and sometimes it's really hard to focus with everything vying for attention…but I feel like I got distracted with the road I went down with this one (which, inadvertently proved my point).

The Magnetic One

A surprisingly long time ago
I went out one December night
And met the magnetic one
The matching polarity, that,
Like two passing neutron stars
Spun around each other's orbit
Like souls predestined to meet
With concentrated gravity pulling,
Embracing, grouped permanently
These two powerful electromagnets
Destined. Found. Together.

                    December 24, 2018
                    Whately, Massachusetts

Kari.

Last Night

When cities have events
On New Year's Eve
Why are they called
"First Night"
When something like
"Last Night"
Would be
Much more appropriate
Because it's not like
They're having the event
On the night
Of New Year's Day
Which would, at least,
Make a lot more sense
Maybe it's more of a
Looking-forward
Kind of a thing
Like a "this year is over
So let's instead
Focus on this new thing
That's tomorrow
But we're going
To celebrate it today,"
Kind of a thing
Which, I guess
Makes sense

Sort of.

December 31, 2018
Whately, Massachusetts

Just something I was thinking about today.

Tomorrow Will Be The Same

When given the choice
Of where to spend
The last evening of the year
Would I rather be downtown
Squished shoulder-to-shoulder
With thousands of other people
At any of the dozens of
City-wide events, in the rain,
With limited access to things like
Bathrooms, couches, or snacks
Or
Would I rather be in my own home
Spending a quiet evening doing
Whatever I wanted,
Whenever I wanted
And if I felt like going to bed early
It would be completely okay
Since tomorrow will be the same
For all of us when we wake up
On the morning of January 1st

December 31, 2018
Whately, Massachusetts

I'm choosing the latter! And writing poetry between snacks and watching movies.

The Hardest Part

The hardest part is
Conceptualizing
Focusing
Creating
Organizing
Condensing
Editing
The thoughts…
The thousands
Of thoughts
Into something
Coherent
Plausible
Interesting
Compelling
Persuasive
Fascinating
Absorbing;
Something
Worth spending
Months, or years,
Writing
Thereby perfecting
Something
Entertaining
Worth spending
A few hours reading

December 31, 2018
Whately, Massachusetts

Writing.

Stop Rowing

When you focus on the big picture
And are immediately faced with
Logistics too deep to consider
Sometimes it's a lot easier
To stop rowing and surrender
To the overly complex nature
Of the swirls, eddies, and vortices
To just go with the flow and just see
Where you'll end up because it might be
That the Universe will deliver you
Someplace never even considered
That's a hundred million times better
Than the place you originally had in mind

December 31, 2018
Whately, Massachusetts

I normally don't like to rhyme this much, but I like it.

New Year's Eve Way Of Seeing Things

When I look back on where I was
Just one single year ago
Physically, mentally, geographically
At the end of a dumpster fire of a year
And now here we are
At the end of a landfill fire of a year
The details of which you already know
If you had access to news (real or fake)
But I digress
Because the place I was at
On this same date in 2017
Was so radically different
From where I'm at now
Having moved a thousand miles
Changed regions, states,
Towns and license plates
Exchanged one way of living
For another completely
One where I'm welcomed
One with more opportunity
One full of creativity
And open-mindedness
Not just for me, but for everybody.
Sure, some aspects of the transition
Have been tough and difficult
But loving my *place*
The location where I choose to BE
This comforting incubator of inspiration
Where I have decided to call my home
And my place within it
And the scenic view I have of the future
That goes on as far as the eye can see
Full of every kind of everything
Which makes me beam with pride
And appreciate the hills that hug
This preciously perfect place
And it is at this point on the calendar

At the very end is when
One is most likely
To look back
To look forward
And generally look around a lot
And make an effort to take stock
Of the quality of life in general
Which is why I enjoy this annual
New Year's Eve way of seeing things
A moment of reflection and recognition
Before heading full-on into next year

December 31, 2018
Whately, Massachusetts

Happy (almost) New Year!

December

IF YOU ENJOYED THIS COLLECTION

Please consider rating it at Amazon.com. As an independent author, having people review my works is critical in helping to increase my exposure and letting new people discover books like this. Thank you!

WRITTEN BY ERIC NIXON

Equidistant – 2018 poetry collection
The Cupcake – 2017 poetry collection
2492: Attack Of The Ancient Cyborg – science fiction novel
The Ocean Above – 2016 poetry collection
Cascadia's Fault – 2015 poetry collection
The Taborist – 2014 poetry collection
The Entire Universe – 2013 poetry collection
Trying Not To Blink – 2012 poetry collection
Emily Dickinson – Superhero: Vol. 1 – historical fiction novel
Lost In Thought – poetry collection
Incident On The Hennepin – a short story set in *2492*
Plenty Of Time – a short story
Retribution On A Jetpack – a short story set in *2492*
Anything But Dreams – poetry collection

Available at Amazon.com/author/ericnixon

ABOUT THE AUTHOR

Eric Nixon is the poet and author of nine collections of poetry, several short stories, and two novels. Eric lives with his author wife, Kari Chapin, in western Massachusetts.

Made in the USA
San Bernardino, CA
10 September 2019